BROKEN PATTERNS

The Education
of a Quarterback

by
FRAN TARKENTON

as told to

BROCK YATES

SIMON AND SCHUSTER | NEW YORK

First printing

SBN 671-21053-X
Library of Congress Catalog Card Number: 76-159137
Designed by Edith Fowler
Manufactured in the United States of America

BROKEN PATTERNS

I

THERE ARE no sports stories in New York, only sagas, epics and legends. You have to be aware of this before you can understand the impact of New York on a professional athlete and most especially on those premier positions such as center fielder for the New York Yankees, where a man gets to frolic around among the monuments with the spirits of DiMaggio and Mantle matching him stride for stride, or as quarterback of the Giants, a position that can sometimes make a player feel more like the keeper of the flame than a signal caller and pass thrower.

New York is the media capital of the United States, home of NBC, CBS and ABC television, the four major radio networks, Associated Press and United Press International, most of the big-buck ad agencies, a substantial percentage of the nation's book and magazine publishers and enough writers, photographers, artists, cinematographers, producers, directors, editors and journalists to glut the world with sensory inputs for the next hundred years. Everything that happens in the city, and most especially the major league sports scene, is placed under a giant arc light for examination and dissection. All that corn about the Big Apple and Gotham, the Great White Way and the Crossroads of the World, is still a part of the New York syndrome. Tom Wolfe, the essayist, zeroed in on this mentality in a piece he called "The Big League Complex." Just as everybody west of Rosemead, California, secretly thinks he's a movie star, every guy east of Newark *knows* he's a major leaguer.

A majority of the national sports commentary in the United States, from the syndicated newspaper drollery of Red Smith, to the abrasive candor of Howard Cosell, to the semantic stunt-flying of Heywood Hale Broun, emanates from New York. These men live within a legend, chained to the ghosts of Grantland Rice, Damon Runyan and Stanley Woodward; tethered to the proposition that the games they witness and report upon are at the very least monumental. To do otherwise would demean themselves and the city's big league complex. Because these men and hundreds like them hover over the local sports scene like so many communications satellites, ready to beam the news to the provinces, New York assumes an exaggerated importance in the national sports picture. After all, these guys aren't about to report on *just games.* When they show up, it better be important. As for the players, they better plan on being anything but average— heroes are O.K., bums are just fine—and they better figure it were as if they had never picked up a stick or a ball until they got to New York. Y. A. Tittle, for example, labored with vast skill for years with the Baltimore Colts and the San Francisco 49ers and didn't come to the Giants until he was thirty-five years old. But his tenure with the Giants brought him the same kind of exposure as if he'd reached town straight from the Louisiana State University campus. Y. A. Tittle was a *new* football player when he arrived in New York. Countless other sports heroes from Babe Ruth to Joe Namath, have become international celebrities in a large part because of their exposure by the New York press. (Babe starred for six years with the Boston Red Sox before reaching the Yankees, but who remembers?) There are many who will argue that Honus Wagner was a greater ball player than ol' Babe, but whoever got famous in Pittsburgh besides Andrew Carnegie? As for Namath, it is possible that the American Football League would never have survived if the entire episode (or should I say epic?) of Broadway Joe, his $400,000 and his bad knees hadn't taken place. After all, I can name you a bunch of quarterbacks who are at least as talented as Namath and any number of guys in the league who are bigger swingers. What is more, both Donnie Anderson and Jim Grabowski got more money for signing with the Green Bay Packers than did Joe. And poor old Bill Nelsen of Cleveland has worse knees than Namath ever had in his grimmest nightmare. But how many wire services and nationally syndicated newspaper columnists are based in Cleveland and Green Bay? It is said that an old All-American Conference, which operated from 1946 to 1949 before merging with the NFL, failed solely because it couldn't sustain a successful team in New York, and I think it's more than coincidence that the American Football League gained the breath of life only after the hopeless New York Titans were replaced by Sonny Werblin's tougher, tighter Jets organization and Broadway Joe turned them into winners on the field and at the gate.

As a matter of fact, the impact of the Jets and Namath on the New York sports scene had some bearing on my coming to the Giants. Those were the days of the savage rivalry between the NFL and the AFL, and if the Jets and their league were to make it, it would have to be at the expense of the Giants and our league. In a sense, the entire struggle between the two pro football forces was acted out between the fortress-like bastions of Yankee Stadium in the Bronx and Shea Stadium, a few miles to the east on the windswept shoreline of

Queens. If the American League could establish a beachhead in New York, its chances for success were excellent. At the same time, it was imperative that the Giants maintain their image as one of the most powerful, prestigious franchises in the older National Football League. Although the dispute could never be resolved by anything so simple as a showdown scrimmage to determine which team would rule New York and which would leave town, the struggle was to be carried out in terms of the exposure each team received from the big names in the local press and the amount of impact each club had on the television and advertising moguls who viewed the battle from their dusky granite towers in midtown Manhattan.

Although Broadway Joe had never flung a pass over the head of any blue-and-red-helmeted Giant, he had hurt the team and the NFL. When Werblin drafted him in 1964, the NFL knew they were in for a battle for the sports pages. It is no coincidence that the same year brought the American League its first fat television contract. They picked up a five-year deal to televise the AFL games for $34 million—comparable to the two-year price of $14.1 million that CBS was paying for the NFL's regular season games. Joe, in company with a substantial collection of press agents, took New York by storm. Aside from his skill on the field, Namath had a certain ability to communicate with the bedrock New York sports fans—the cabdrivers, waiters, bartenders and cops—who can be the final arbiters of skill in the city. He was their kind of guy. A cocky, loose-limbed kid from Beaver Falls, Pennsylvania, with his tough talk, his wild clothes, his long hair, his white shoes, his wiggy bachelor's pad—*everything* made him the kind of guy that Damon Runyon would have hitchhiked to Poughkeepsie to write about. Every move he made on and off the field generated ink, and for the Giants, he couldn't have come at a worse time.

You've got to remember that in 1964 the Giants' establishment was the personification of the fusty, smug National Football League. They were a fixture in the city, like Grant's Tomb—and at that particular moment, just about as exciting. Like their fellow residents of the Bronx, the Yankees, they were as close to an Ivy League team as any professional club can get. They reeked of tradition, and although none of them were enshrined in Yankee Stadium's center field like Ruth and Gehrig, men like the great Tim Mara, Mel Hein, Tuffy Leemans, Cal Hubbard, Ken Strong and Steve Owen, loomed in the mists of the 1930s and 1940s. The Giants were participants in the NFL Championship game in 1933—the year professional football is supposed to have emerged as an authentic major league sport. They lost, 23–21, but went on to play in more title games than any other team and to win championships in 1934, 1938 and 1956.

The 1950s brought the legendary defense led by Sam Huff, Andy Robustelli and Emlen Tunnell, and a gutsy attack starring aging Charley Conerly and a pair of stylish westerners, Kyle Rote and Frank Gifford. This decade established the murderous rivalry with the powerful Cleveland Browns and made New York host to the single game that did more to generate interest in pro football than any other event. That of course was the unforgettable 23–17 overtime victory by the Colts over the Giants in Yankee Stadium in 1958. There it was, right in Gotham, the only NFL championship game in history to go into sudden death, and it had to happen in front of the notebooks, microphones and television cameras of the nation's most powerful sporting press. Pro football was on its way to becoming the national craze and I knew I wanted to be a part of the action.

I can remember watching that game at my folks' home in
Athens, Georgia. I was a struggling sophomore quarterback
at the University of Georgia, laboring in the shadows of the
multitalented Charley Britt and wondering if I'd ever have a
chance to make the pros. Actually basketball was my best
sport, but I knew I was too short for the NBA. I'd popped a
tendon in my right forearm while pitching in high school, so
major league baseball was out, and that left me with one
sports fantasy—playing quarterback for the Washington Redskins. Yep, the Redskins. I'd lived there between the ages of
five and eleven and was really into the sports scene—Bones
McKinney and the Capitols basketball team; the Senators
with Stan Spence and Mickey Vernon, and most of all, the
Redskins and Slingin' Sammy Baugh. I mean, I was really
into the Redskins. I could sing every stanza of "Hail to the
Redskins," and when we left town, moving to Georgia, I can
remember gazing back at the city from the Fourteenth Street
Bridge and giving it the General MacArthur number about
"I shall return."

I nurtured that dream until I was a senior, when a friend
of mine told me he had received word from George Preston
Marshal, patriarchal owner of the 'Skins, that I would be
drafted number one. I was delirious. Fantasy fulfilled! Then
I got word at the Blue-Gray game that my good friend Norm
Snead had gone to Washington in the first round and me—
I'd been neglected until the third round, when a new team
up in Minnesota called the Vikings had finally dragged me
off the scrap heap (I thought then that any quarterback
worth anything at all *had* to go in the first round). I felt lousy
about the Redskins' rejection until my backfield coach at
Georgia, Charlie Trippi, who'd been a great with the Cardinals, told me it was the luckiest thing that ever happened

to me. "Washington is the worst franchise in the National Football League," he said flatly.

That, I didn't know at the time of the 1958 Colts-Giants encounter, although I did root for New York. After all, how could I support the Colts? They were the arch enemies of the Redskins.

From 1958 through 1963 the Giants won five Eastern Conference championships and their power in the national sports establishment was unquestioned. Their games were sold out, with season tickets as hard to come by as an invitation to the White House. Before NFL Commissioner Pete Rozelle divided the television revenue equally among the league members, the Giants commanded three times as much money as any other franchise. Names like Walton, Thomas, Gifford, Grier, Stroud, Brown, Shofner, Dess, Larson, Webster, King, Morrison, Katcavage, Robustelli, Lovetere, Modzelewski, Scott, Livingston, Lynch, Barnes, Patton and Chandler were memorized in a litany of Giant heroics. Names like Tittle and Huff were worshiped.

The Giant power had been welded together by a series of excellent coaches, beginning with Steve Owen, who is credited with a major role in developing modern pass defenses as early as 1950. A key figure in his four-man "umbrella" secondary —created largely to stop Otto Graham and the Cleveland Browns—was Tom Landry, who ended a fine playing career in the middle fifties to become the Giants' defensive coach. When Owen retired he was replaced by Jim Lee Howell, a cool administrator and over-all tactician who left his defense to Landry and his offense to a squat, tough-talking football genius named Vince Lombardi. Because of their excellent records with the Giants, Landry was hired as head coach of the Dallas Cowboys when they entered the league in 1960, and Lombardi of course went on to immortality at Green Bay. When Howell stepped down in 1961, he handed control to Allie Sherman, an offensive assistant. The team continued to win. However, the personnel had remained relatively stable since the NFL championship year of 1956, and very little new blood had been injected into the team. The Giants continued to dominate the Eastern Conference but always fell short of the title, and the frustration, both among their fans and among their aging players, was becoming unbearable.

The 1963 game hurt the most. The Giants had gone 11–3 in the regular season, winning the Eastern Conference by a game over the hated Browns. Tittle, who was thirty-eight years old, took the Giants into chill Wrigley Field in Chicago to face the Bears—a team that had lost but one game and tied two in the West, thanks to a rockbound defense that had allowed a skimpy 144 points to be scored against them in the regular season. They had to be tough, because the Bears' offense was as weak as any championship team's in history. Led by Billy Wade, who was not considered a first-rate quarterback, the Bears squeezed into the Western Conference title while scoring only 301 points in fourteen games. The Giants, having lost the NFL playoff to Green Bay the two previous years, figured to win. Y. A. had directed an offense that had produced 448 points during the regular season (among the very best total in league history) and had won the passing championship himself with 36 touchdown passes. In fact, the 39 passing TDs registered by the 1963 Giants is an NFL record. The team led the league in total yards gained and kicker Don Chandler, who was at the peak of his career, produced 106 points to win the NFL individual scoring championship. These impressive statistics, coupled with the poised, well-drilled Giant defense, which had sacked the opposing quarterback fifty-seven times during the regular season, made

it a reasonable assumption that the New Yorkers could overcome the Bears and their powder-puff offense. After all, how
many points can a defense score?

Fourteen, as it turned out, and that was enough to win.

The Bears' three magnificent linebackers, Bill George,
Larry Morris and Joe Fortunato, operated in perfect concert
with safeties Roosevelt Taylor and Richie Petitbon that afternoon and intercepted five of Y. A.'s passes. Two of them were
picked off close enough to the Giants' goal line to permit even
the feeble Bear attack to get the ball over. The impenetrable
Bear pass defense blunted the unstoppable Giant attack and
won the game 14–10.

The Giants returned home in despair. They had entered
five NFL championship games in six years and lost each time.
The New York press was furious. Tittle was questioned as
being over the hill. The defense was criticized for not trying
hard enough. The world's greatest heroes were capable of
being nothing but the world's greatest bums.

The months following that game, I think, had a direct
effect not only on my coming to the New York Giants but my
impact on the team after arriving. Allie Sherman made a mistake, albeit an honest one, that overcomes most coaches from
time to time. He felt that it is coaching that makes great football teams, not great personnel. He had a number of established names on his roster and they were put up for trade.
Sherman felt that some of his stars were getting a bit long
in the tooth and some sharp trading would bring in youngsters who could be coached to carry on the Giants' winning
ways. At that point he made the one error that was to drive
both the Giants and Sherman himself into decline.

I doubt that most New Yorkers believed the headlines. It
made no sense when they read that their beloved Sam Huff
had been traded to Washington. The outcry was instantane-

ous, as if the city had in fact sold the Brooklyn Bridge. You've got to realize that Sam Huff was one of the biggest heroes in the history of New York sports. But that unto itself wasn't the problem; the Giants could have withstood the fans' anger if the trade had brought a net gain in team strength. It did not. Aside from being an authentic star, Sam was a tremendous team-leader. He was popular among his fellows, and a rallying point for the defense in moments of extreme stress. Although the coaching staff didn't think Sam was playing at top form, he, like all great stars, was still capable of effecting the course of any game in which he played. Everybody liked Sam Huff, and the depressing effect his departure had on the team's spirit cannot be calculated. It took the starch out of them, just as if Joe DiMaggio or John Unitas had been bartered away during their prime years. The internal damage this did to Sherman's reputation within the Giant establishment—the players themselves, the retired team members, the hangers-on, favored members of the press, etc.—was immense and in some ways it is a miracle Allie managed as well as he did in the years to come.

The Huff trade was like opening a coal chute. From that moment on, nothing worked. To get the great middle linebacker the Redskins gave up Dickie James, a jack-of-all-trades runner and pass receiver who had lost his speed, and Andy Stynchula, a defensive lineman who was past his prime and did not want to play in New York. Neither contributed anything notable to the Giants' cause. To compound the trouble, Sherman traded Dick Modzelewski, a powerful defensive lineman who, like Huff, was a team leader. He went to Cleveland for a modestly talented tight end named Bob Crespino, who never started for the Giants. Running back Phil King went to the Steelers for an inconsequential draft choice. Phil later went to Minnesota and had his third-best year in pro ball.

The 1964 season found the Giants decimated. The loss of Huff and Modzelewski, plus the retirement of several key veterans, sailed the team into last place in the Eastern Conference with a shocking 2-10-2 record. Tittle was injured at midseason and young Gary Wood, a gutsy but inexperienced kid from Cornell, simply couldn't turn the team around. Added to that, some of the all-time Giant greats like Frank Gifford, Jim Patton and Andy Robustelli were at the end of their careers and just couldn't play at their peak anymore. John Lovetere, a fine defensive stalwart, hurt his knee. Don Chandler was mysteriously traded to the Packers, for a worthless, middle-round draft choice. Alex Webster, a tower of strength both physically and emotionally for the Giants, was gone and there was nobody to take his place.

Frantically, Allie reshuffled his few remaining stars. Tittle's eyesight was giving him problems, but he wanted to keep playing. However, Y. A. could see that the upcoming years were going to be nightmares. Unbelievably, relieving Gary Wood in a late 1964 game, he had been booed by the Giant fans! He announced his retirement in early 1965 and Sherman made no effort to change his mind. Allie traded Darrell Dess, an all-Pro offensive guard, and Erich Barnes, one of the toughest cornerbacks in football. Barnes was traded to Cleveland for linebacker Mike Lucci, who was immediately re-traded with Dess, to the Detroit Lions for quarterback Earl Morrall. (Darrell was to return later.) Ironically Barnes's arrival in Cleveland galvanized the Browns defense around the two ex-Giants, Barnes and Modzelewski and helped propel them to the NFL Championship!

Morrall had floated around the league up to then, having

failed to find a home with Pittsburgh, San Francisco and Detroit, but he was an experienced quarterback who helped the Giants in 1965. Somehow, operating with a skeleton crew of hobbled veterans and unproven youngsters, Morrall managed to bring the Giants home with a won-seven, lost-seven record. In retrospect, they were lucky to have been operating in the Eastern Conference, which was laden with weak teams that year. In fact, only one team of the seven won more than it lost.

As if to underscore the shocking collapse of the dynasty, the team had made atrocious use of its draft choices. Lee Grosscup, Glynn Griffing and Bob Timberlake all came to the club with dazzling college records and at one time or another looked like prime candidates to take over the starting quarterback assignment. But like George Shaw, who had swept into town from a Rookie of the Year triumph with the Baltimore Colts appearing to be a sure bet to replace Charley Conerly, none of them remotely challenged for the job. After Shaw had been traded to the Vikings, Grosscup had a brief moment of glory, fascinating the local press with his intellectual powers but depressing the coaching staff with his inability to throw the football. It was at this point that the Giants had their only turn of good fortune. San Francisco had given up on Y. A. Tittle in favor of two young studs named John Brodie and Billy Kilmer and they traded him to New York—and stardom—for Lou Cordileone, an overrated lineman. But the draft continued to be a dry well for the Giants. Glynn Griffing came to them with the entire state of Mississippi ready to testify that he was the greatest football player in history. Again, a variety of troubles prevented him from making the big time. Timberlake arrived from Michigan with All-American accolades and credit for a Rose Bowl victory, but he ended up doing no more than some utility kicking and finally disappeared. Ironically, Bob finally used his Giant contract money to help finance his studies at the Princeton Divinity school.

Joe Don Looney blew in from Oklahoma with credentials to become another Jimmy Brown. Endowed with great physical skills, Joe simply could not adjust emotionally to the regimens of pro ball and was traded to the Colts for Andy Nelson, a defensive back and R. C. Owens, a flanker. Both had been starters, both were over the hill, both retired without helping the Giants. Tucker Frederickson very nearly lost his chance with the team as well. After magnificent rookie running in 1965, during which he gained 659 yards, a terrible knee injury took him out of the lineup for the entire next year—a period in which the Giants hit bottom. With his old horses out to pasture and his prime draft choices a ragged army of misfits, no-talents and walking wounded, Sherman found he had no bargaining power left. Nobody wanted to trade with him and he simply didn't have the personnel available to win football games. Then Morrall broke a bone in his right hand in the middle of the season and the job was turned over to Gary Wood and briefly to youthful Tom Kennedy. It was legalized murder.

During the dark months of the autumn of 1966, the New York Giants, former titans of the National Football League, played fourteen games. They won one. Somehow they managed to tie another. The defense, or at least the eleven men who appeared on the field when the other team had the ball and were generously referred to as the defense, yielded 501 points. That is a record that stands for all professional football and will probably remain unchallenged for years to come. In one particularly depressing display, the Giants gave up 72 points in one sixty-minute encounter with the Redskins (featuring, ironically, Sam Huff at middle linebacker). It was a disaster and the New York press corps was treating the whole thing like the Fall of Rome. The fans pitched in by composing a curt chant that lamented, "Good-bye, Allie."

Meanwhile, over in Queens, Broadway Joe and the Jets were breezing along to six victories (in a lackluster division, it should be noted) while tying two and attracting excellent crowds—nothing like the Giant's packed houses, but with the clown act in Yankee Stadium, how long could the NFL maintain credibility in New York? The Giants, as the stand-ard-bearers of the National Football League and the proud football representatives of America's greatest city, were about ready to take refuge with their farm team, the West-chester Bulls.

The big hole—or at least the hole the press and the fans were yelling most about—was at quarterback. They wanted a hero behind center. Their desires of course oversimplified the problem, because any team that is planning to give up more than 500 points in the season shouldn't plan on winning even with a combination of Jim Thorpe, Frank Merriwell and Dink Stover in the backfield and Horatio Alger writing the game plans. On the other hand, the likes of an injured Morrall and Wood simply left the Giants undermanned, both on the field and in the local papers, where Mr. Namath was producing winning headlines, if not winning scores. The Giants management, led by Wellington Mara and seconded by Sherman, knew they had to have a different quarterback if they were going to compete with *anybody* in New York.

It's interesting to note that the Giants have never been able to function with a young or unestablished quarterback. Charley Conerly, who played until he was in his early forties, learned to ignore the fan's boos that thundered throughout

Yankee Stadium and to lead winning teams. He was not a picture-book quarterback by any means; his passes tended to wobble and he was a slow man afoot. But Charley Conerly was a great team-leader and his coolness under fire—both from the opposing teams and his hometown crowd—made him a winner. And in the final analysis, that is a powerful measurement of greatness. Y. A. Tittle came to New York with 13 years in the pros behind him. He was supremely confident of his skills and had the advantage of being able to step into the leadership of an abundantly talented team. Nevertheless, it is doubtful if a younger, less mature player could have handled the job, simply because of the immense pressure exerted in the New York sports scene. Maybe Grosscup, Griffing, *et al*, weren't as bad as they looked.

The sad experiences with Gary Wood (who might very well have made it in a situation in which there hadn't been such instantaneous demands on his skills) and Earl Morrall, whose record with Baltimore after leaving New York in 1968 removes any doubt about his qualifications to play quarterback, seemed to emphasize the point that a special kind of personality was needed to play that position for the New York Giants. Wellington Mara and Allie Sherman, for one reason or another, were willing to gamble that I could take it. I believed I could too, although I'll be dead honest; I'm not sure I'd have been tough enough if I'd have been a kid of twenty-two or twenty-three. When I came to the Giants I'd had six years of pro ball. I'd been booed, I'd fumbled, I'd thrown disastrous interceptions, I'd done every dumb thing on a football field a pro quarterback is capable of doing. I had heard over and over how scrambling couldn't win in the NFL and how I was too cute and clever as a runner for my own good. That didn't bother me anymore.

But if I'd been a green kid out of Georgia struggling to make it with the New York Giants, who were trying to lift themselves off the canvas after a nine count, the whole thing just might have cracked me.

II

———————————————

A GUY TOLD ME once, "Whatever you're going to be in New York, you're going to be a lot more than anywhere else. If you're going to be a hero, you'll be a bigger hero than anywhere else; and if you're going to be a bum, you'll be a bigger bum than anywhere else."

Good advice. Especially for quarterbacks on the New York Giants.

I didn't really understand that principle of magnification when I arrived in town from the friendly, frozen expanses of Minnesota in 1967. I only knew that I was moving into a period of uncertainty of my career and the job with the Giants would make me or break me. It may sound ridiculous coming from a red-clay and sunshine Georgia boy, but I had loved Minnesota. My wife, Elaine, and I had settled into the relaxed life of Minneapolis and our roots were growing deep. Despite my simmering feud with the then Vikings coach, Norm Van Brocklin, I was totally involved with the team. I had been, for all intents and purposes, their only quarterback. Beginning with that insanely improbable 37–13 over the Chicago Bears in the Vikings' first league game, in 1961, we had struggled—often with more spirit than skill— through four seasons of the zany peaks and valleys that are so typical of a youthful expansion team—to a point where we could see championships in the middle distance. We had the nucleus of an imposing defense built around Carl Eller and Jim Marshall at the ends and quality linebackers like Roy Winston and Lonnie Warwick. A pair of superb running backs named Tommy Mason and Bill Brown, plus All-Pro linemen Mick Tingelhoff and Grady Alderman and receiver Paul Flatley, gave us an authentically potent offense as well as visions that it was no longer pure fantasy that an NFL title would come to Minnesota.

By 1965 we were gaining momentum at a furious rate. Our season opened with five straight exhibition victories. That in itself was not unusual for the Vikings. At one point we won seventeen straight pre-season games, thanks I suppose to the urgings of Van Brocklin, who managed to get us so lathered up for these contests that we played each one as if the entire fate of Western Civilization hung in the balance. Then, with the regular season about to open, he would announce, "All right, you guys, now we play for *real!*"

But we'd already been playing for real, operating at an emotional peak, and his revelation always brought a letdown. For example, in 1965 we bombed Dallas in the next-to-last exhibition game 57–16—and those guys were on their way to an NFL title shot with Green Bay the next year! Then came the "real" season. A few hours before we opened against the Colts, Phil King, a rangy runner who had played on three Eastern Conference Championship teams with the Giants before coming to the Vikings, said to me, "Wow, I feel more pressure on me now than in any of the title games I played with the Giants, and we're only beginning!" Baltimore put us away 35–16 and we lost our next one to Detroit 31–29 when Milt Plum completed a pass out of what seemed like deep left field with thirty seconds remaining. Here were

the Minnesota Vikings, the best young team in football, pre-
dicted by some to beat the Packers for their division title,
winless in our first two games and thoroughly frustrated.

We could score, but we couldn't prevent getting scored
upon. Our games were like a sprint race with each team
scurrying to run up more points on the board than the other
before the clock ran out. We beat Los Angeles 38–35 on a
last-minute field goal by Fred Cox, then blew the Giants out
of the park 40–14. The Chicago game was more like our
style, when Gale Sayers scored four touchdowns to lead the
Bears to a 45–37 victory. The following week we spotted San
Francisco a 21–0 lead, then struggled back to win 42–41.
(And those were the days when they were snickering about
the basketball scores being rung up in the rival American
Football League.) Anyway, we dumped the Rams a second
time, then stopped Jimmy Brown and Cleveland cold and,
with a 5–3 record, got ready for round two with the Colts.
If we stabilized ourselves, we still had a shot at the Western
title.

Van Brocklin decided to start rookie Earsell Mackbee at
left cornerback—a likable kid the Vikings had signed as a
free agent. It was Earsell's job to cover Jimmy Orr of the
Colts, who was a handful for even the best defensive backs
in the league. Presumably Mackbee's job would be made
slightly easier because John Unitas was out with an arm
injury and would be replaced with Gary Cuozzo. We shoved
the Colts around in the first half and were thinking about
holding a 7–3 halftime lead when Orr scooted 15 yards behind Mackbee, and Cuozzo nailed him with a 50-yard scoring pass. Somehow the touchdown took the starch out of us
and we were useless in the second half. What's more, Orr got
Mackbee's number and he caught repeated passes for big
yardage and touchdowns. With the score mounting (we

finally lost 41–21, Cuozzo throwing five touchdown passes), our defensive coach, Jack Faulkner tried to take the heat off Mackbee by getting Dutch to switch to a zone defense. I'll never forget Van Brocklin's answer, "Nope, let 'em beat the nigger."

The next morning Van Brocklin called a surprise press conference for a few of the key Minneapolis-area sports-writers and said, "I've taken this football team as far as I can. Effective right now, I'm resigning as coach of the Minnesota Vikings." The word passed around town like news of a third World War. Along with my roommate, defensive co-captain Rip Hawkins, I was called into a conference with the club's major stockholders, Bernie Ridder and Max Winter, and the general manager, Jim Finks. They tried to get Rip and me to talk with Dutch in hopes of persuading him to return. I said, "I think Rip will agree with me when I say that it won't work. The team is bigger than all of us—the owners, the players and the coaches. There's going to be a Viking team after we're all gone. As far as I'm concerned, he's made his stand. He's a big boy and I don't think any of the guys on the team could respect him if he came back." Rip agreed. I didn't bother to say that most of the players were cheering the word and at that moment some of them were gathering at the Rand Bar in St. Paul to begin a cele-bration. Nothing was resolved and the meeting broke up after Ridder said, "I think Norm's slipped a bolt somewhere."

The following day, just as I was getting out of bed, Jim Finks called me to report that an all-night session had con-vinced Norm to return. Practice that day was wild. The players bordered on open revolt. Except for Phil King and Bill Barnes, a pair of backs, the team was unanimous in wanting Rip and me to notify Van Brocklin that we simply would not play for him. We talked them out of such a move, but they were really sore. They'd never really liked Van Brocklin, but that wasn't important. Norm had driven them hard and you don't have to like a coach to play for him, but there has to be respect. Norm had lost that, and there was no way it could be recovered. The rest of the season was hopeless and we were lucky to get out of it with a 7–7 record. Another year of great expectations for Norm and the Vikings had squirted past.

A lot has been written about the feud between Van Brocklin and myself, but I think it should be made clear that our relationship was reasonably pleasant for most of my stay with the Vikings. The fact was, save for a couple of outbursts of temper that are bound to happen among highly competitive men, we didn't have much trouble working with each other. Norm Van Brocklin taught me pro football, make no mistake about that. He taught me how to read defenses, how to attack a team, how to exploit their weaknesses, how to nullify their strengths, how to win.

Norm was an old-time pro—an ex-Navy man, cocky, tough-talking, overbearing, intensely competitive. You could not maintain a neutral opinion about Dutch; you either loved him or hated him and I flip-flopped between the two emotions countless times while I was with him. When he was up and at his sharpest, he was the best leader of men I'd ever met. When he was down, depressed, feeling beaten, he could be one of the surliest, nastiest-tempered men on earth. Only a man like Van Brocklin could swagger into Philadelphia and announce, "The Eagles were nothing before I came here and they'll be nothing after I leave." In 1960 he led them out of nowhere to win the NFL Championship, then retired. Since then the Eagles have had only two winning seasons. That sort of energy got him into the Hall of Fame. But his hair-trigger temper and his big mouth made him so visible around the league that other teams weren't playing us, the Minnesota Vikings; they were carrying out some weird personal combat with ol' Dutch. And he loved it.

I can recall my first exhibition game against Dallas, in Sioux Falls, South Dakota. Here I was, a wet-eared kid out of Georgia, witnessing a genuine pro game from the sidelines. On the opening series of downs the Cowboys moved the ball to midfield, where their flanker, Frank Clarke lined up near our bench. Suddenly Dutch was leaping up and down, practically screaming in Clarke's ear, "Clarke, you pussy! You ——— stiff, you blankety-blank-blank . . .!" I couldn't believe it; here was a professional coach hollering at one of the Cowboys like a drunken heckler in a sandlot game. All I could assume was that Clarke had somehow perpetrated some awful deed against Dutch and they were mortal enemies. But the following week he did the same thing with Baltimore's great flanker Lenny Moore, and I began to get the message: Dutch was so competitive he assaulted the opposition with *everything,* including his vocal cords.

Later that season we were playing the 49ers, a team Dutch despised almost as much as his old Rams club. He was in a lather before the game started, pacing up and down the locker room with his tongue playing against his lips—a sure sign Dutch was mad. They punted to us and one of our guys charged in and knocked their kicker into a heap. Flags flew everywhere, but Hugh McElhenny, our magnificent veteran, caught the ball and made one of his patented open-field runs through the 49ers for a touchdown. Of course it was called back, and I heard this explosion of words from Dutch. As the official was walking off our 15-yard penalty, Van Brocklin thundered onto the field, yelling a furious protest to the man in the striped shirt. The referee stopped his walk-off for a moment, coolly regarded Dutch's hollering, then marched off another 15 yards! Dutch stalked off the field, having given the Vikings one of the few 30-yard penalties in the annals of football.

These outbursts of temper could be hilarious, but I don't think Dutch ever realized how he affected the people he assaulted. One day during my second year we were watching game films and the screen displayed one of my dumber scramble plays. I was zooming around the backfield, looking for a receiver, when I sighted Paul Flatley about 40 yards downfield. Off balance, I flung the ball in his direction and it embarked on a serene, floating trajectory more like that of a punt than of a pass. I'm sure poor Paul was expecting to make a fair catch when half the other team piled on him. Van Brocklin turned off the projector, snapped on the room lights and said to me, "Tarkenton, you aren't strong enough to throw a pass like that, but you sure as hell are dumb enough!"

But sometimes Dutch could really hurt his players. Red Phillips came to our team in a trade with Los Angeles with a reputation as a superb pass receiver. Sadly, Red had contracted an extremely serious disease that had stiffened his fingers, and only tremendous will and personal courage kept him playing. Hours of therapy were all that allowed Red on the field, and his tenacity and determination were a source of inspiration for the entire team. Considering his ailment, Red played effectively for us, and we knew lesser men would have given up. Then, during a film session late in the season, a play in which Red dropped a touchdown pass was projected. Again Dutch stopped the movie. "Phillips," he said, "I never thought you'd be one to come here and play out the year."

The whole team wanted to cry—and to let Dutch have one right in his fat mouth.

I don't think Dutch really meant such things. He operated so much on impulse that he tended to say things that other men only thought. He didn't really mean that Red Phillips was a quitter. He didn't really mean Earsell Mackbee was a "nigger," Frank Clarke wasn't a "pussy," all the All-Pro defensive backfields I had to pass against weren't "a gang of stiffs"—that was just ol' sailor Dutch, out front with all that blowhard stuff that made him such a tough man to beat on the football field.

Dutch was forever calling people to apologize for what he'd said to them at cocktail parties the night before. He was also known to phone his players in the middle of the night and bawl them out for something or another. When he was in high spirits, he could be a beautiful man and, I swear, we all loved him. When things were bad (which we could never predict) he could be despicable. He tended to keep us in a frenzy, and for borderline players and rookies a season with Dutch could take years off their lives.

He and I were both take-charge guys and I suppose a clash was inevitable. Our first battle came, I think, on a flight home from a game we'd lost during the 1964 season. I was playing gin with some friends when Dutch came up to our seats and said to me, "Tarkenton, you earn enough money here?"

He had a dark scowl on his face and I knew I was in for something. "Yeah," I replied defiantly.

"Well, you don't deserve a damn cent of it. You're selfish and you're only worried about yourself and not the team."

I threw down my cards and stood up to confront him face to face. "Listen, if you don't like the way I'm playing, trade me. Otherwise, shut your mouth."

As I gained maturity and confidence as a pro, I simply refused to knuckle under to Dutch's abuse. Sometimes our struggles got pretty childish. I can recall more than one instance when Dutch and I stood on the sidelines and shouted at each other:

"———— you."

"———— you!"

"———— *you!*"

"———— *you!*"

As my pal Bill Curry says, that sort of thing is bound to happen when grown men play a kid's game.

Despite absurd confrontations like that, Dutch and I were able to function on a workable player-coach basis until 1965. Then we began to grow apart, to some extent because I was beginning to rival him for exposure as a so-called Vikings "personality." Up until then he'd been the dominant figure on the team, both to the public and to the players, but now I was beginning to rival him on both fronts and that hurt our relationship. He began to tell his friends that I was taking my scrambling too seriously, that I was getting too cute on the field and that this spotlight seeking was hurting the team. He told the press "a scrambler can't win championships," and that remark has haunted me ever since. Meanwhile I was telling my friends that each day I became more convinced that Dutch was a fat-head who opened his mouth only to change feet. Both of us were wrong, but once the wound was opened, it was rubbed. We had two other quarterbacks on the 1966 club, Bob Berry and Ron VanderKelen, both of whom had plenty of potential but were unqualified, I thought, for Dutch's vocal proclamations that they were going to be a pair of the great stars of football. These guys are superstars of the future, he kept telling members of the press. So with five games left and the Vikings still groping along with a chance to win our division, Dutch suddenly announced he was going to start Ron against Los Angeles and Berry against Atlanta.

Los Angeles was weak that year and the Atlanta Falcons were freshmen in the league, so it was possible that we could win with backup quarterbacks, but I was convinced the switch was being made so that Van Brocklin could demonstrate to the world that he didn't need me to win. What's more, the players were sore because they thought the team wasn't being given its best shot and therefore felt Dutch was playing around with their playoff money, which is based on the final standings. They wanted to win, not experiment with new quarterbacks. I had nothing against Ron and Bob in this situation, but I knew they were in for a heap of trouble. Los Angeles beat us 6–3, preventing our offense from scoring a touchdown—and if there was one thing the Vikings could do in those days it was score touchdowns. The following week we played Lombardi's Packers, who were at the height of their power. Dutch put me in for that little frolic, which we lost in a tight battle, but he announced that Bob Berry would start the next game against the Falcons. That really bent me, because I figured part of Dutch's reasoning involved my being a Georgia resident, with a lot of supporters from my college days down there. The game would be televised from Minnesota, with everybody back home wondering what happened to ol' Fran. Berry threw five interceptions and the Falcons, who were an undermanned team, beat us 20–13. That would be my final game in front of the Vikings' home crowd— if you can call riding the bench a "game."

Dutch got some flack from a few of the sportswriters about the Atlanta defeat, then flew off to New York for the National Football Hall of Fame dinner. As far as I can determine, Bernie Ridder must have talked to Van Brocklin on the plane back to Minneapolis about Dutch and me and the open warfare we were about to break into. Every Tuesday morning the Vikings gathered together to discuss the previous game, and Dutch got me to come in early. With just the two of us in his office, and a dark frown on his face, I knew we were in for some heavy going. "Francis" he said dejectedly, "I haven't told this to anybody else, but this is my last year with the Vikings. I'm fed up with coaching and I don't feel I can go any further."

I fumbled around and finally said, "Well, Norm, I wish you luck," although it's entirely possible that Van Brocklin was waiting for me to make a plea for him to stay. He knew I was sore, because following the announcement that he was going to start VanderKelen and Berry, I had gone to him and said, "Listen, it isn't necessary to make a big thing about it, but let me tell you this; I'll run down on kickoffs and I'll run down on punts, anything you want, but if in five weeks I feel the way I do now, I'm not coming back to the team."

This announcement I'm sure had had some effect in getting us together on that particular morning, wherein Dutch got very conciliatory. He told me I should stay with the Vikings, that I had a great deal to contribute to a club that was on the verge of becoming a winner. We talked for a while longer, then broke up to meet the team. That same afternoon, about three o'clock, I got a call at home. It was Dutch and he wanted to see me again. What could he want this time?

He always called me "Francis." When I got to his office, he was slumped behind his desk looking as humble as I'd ever seen him. "Francis, I've been wrong. I just want to tell you I apologize." I had to feel sorry for the guy, because as proud and ballsy as Van Brocklin was, apologizing just wasn't in his makeup. "We've had our differences, but we still want the same thing—to bring a championship here. We've gone through a lot, and what I'd like to do is just wipe the slate clear and start all over."

I was really touched. I loved the whole Vikings scene and this looked as if the one irritant, the weird struggle with Van Brocklin, was finally over. I said, "Norm, there's nothing I'd like better in the world." It was a pretty sentimental scene for a pair of football men. Tears came to Dutch's eyes and he came over and hugged me. For the next hour we had a great talk discussing the things that should be done for the team, etc., in what was the first really relaxed, congenial conversation we'd had in years. When I left I was on top of the world. I knew we had a coming team, and we were finally going to put it all together.

The next day I showed up for practice and Dutch wouldn't speak to me.

I was baffled, dumbstruck. What had happened to yesterday and all that baring of our souls? In retrospect, I think the blowup had come this way: I had four close friends on the Vikings, Grady Alderman, Bill Brown, Mick Tingelhoff and Tommy Mason, and during this whole recent turmoil with Dutch, I'd been frank with them that I wasn't coming back in 1967 if Van Brocklin was still the coach. These guys were friends and I was telling them my honest feelings and not in any way trying to influence them or the rest of the team. The morning after our talk, Van Brocklin had snared Mason before practice and gotten him into his office. Dutch always tended to intimidate Tommy, and for some reason or another had managed to find out that I had said, in effect, that it was he or me in 1967.

Van Brocklin was furious because he assumed I'd been saying this to everybody, including the owners. That wasn't the case, but once Dutch decided something like that, there was no changing his mind. In a rage he called Jim Finks. (In retrospect, the incident is amusing because Van Brocklin's departure from the Los Angeles Rams was based on a "he or me" dictum he had handed down to the owners in a dispute with coach Sid Gillman.

For all intents and purposes, I never spoke to Norm Van Brocklin again that season. I did start against the Detroit Lions the following week and threw three touchdown passes to win 28–16. He seemed to lose interest in the team. For both the Detroit game and our finale with the Bears, he barely involved himself with the strategy. Walt Yowarsky, the Vikings' line coach, put in the running game and end coach Lew Carpenter and I added the passing attack. It worked too, although our defense had more trouble against the Bears and we went down 41–28. I had started my pro career with the Vikings against the Bears and although I didn't know it at the time, I was to finish it against them as well.

I left for my off-season business in Atlanta with the papers foaming with news of the Van Brocklin-Tarkenton blowup. Trade rumors floated around the league. People claimed I was driving hard for a move to New York, where the bright lights and the big buck seemed to have an extraordinary attraction for me. They were wrong. Of course I was thinking about being traded, but the idea of going to Detroit, which seemed on the verge of a championship if they could find more strength at quarterback, or to Chicago, where I could team up with the likes of Gale Sayers and Dick Butkus, intrigued me most. I knew both teams were in the market for a quarterback. So were the Giants, but they seemed to be so weak and floundering so badly that playing with them would just about offset any advantage of operating in New York. The more I thought about it and the more I heard about the growing turmoil in Minnesota, the more I knew I wouldn't return. The thought of playing for Dutch another year was more than I could stand. He had taught me a lot of football and I admitted his vast knowledge of a game, but I had lost respect for him as a coach. At that time, under that pressure, I thought he was the worst human being I knew. I just couldn't lie to my teammates or to him anymore, trying to make them believe I could give Dutch my complete loyalty. I couldn't, and it was over.

I was on may way to Spokane, Washington, in early February, 1967, and planned a two-hour stopover in Minneapolis to lay it on Van Brocklin. I met him at eleven o'clock in the morning and got right into it. "Norm, there's no need for us to get into a lot of name calling contests or a lot of reasons why we're in the situation we're in. We're two adults, but this is it; I'm not coming back here to play."

I thought he'd quickly agree and I'd be on my way, but Van Brocklin became very charming and started to ramble on about football and the future of the Vikings. I delayed my one-o'clock flight out of town and stayed for lunch. The conversation droned on with me trying to make my point and Norm jocularly avoiding the issue. Five hours later I knew the situation was hopeless. We got to joking around, going nowhere, and I left for Spokane with nothing settled. At that moment, for what reason I do not know, he simply wasn't ready to confront the issue.

On the West Coast, I ran into more trade rumors and I knew it was up to me to take some action. The following Monday I put together a letter to Van Brocklin with copies to all the Vikings directors. It said:

Dear Norm,

After much thought, I have come to a definite conclusion that under no circumstances can I return to play football with the Minnesota Vikings next season.

Because of the events of the past few months and my feelings toward a number of things, it is impossible for me to return to the Vikings with a clear and open mind. As you know, I have tried to subdue these feelings and erase them from my mind, but it has been impossible.

Feeling as I do, I am sure this decision is the best for the Vikings, you and myself.

Norm, I sincerely appreciate your help and guidance during the early years of my pro career and I certainly wish for you, and the Vikings, every success.

I hope you and the organization understand that nothing can be done which would change my decision.

Because of all that the organization has done for me, I am writing this letter in the event that it might be helpful to the Vikings to know my feelings at this time.

Sincerely,

Francis A. Tarkenton

That was about as cool as I could keep the language and I thought it made my point without rubbing any of the old wounds. Just to be sure that everything was perfect, I planned to hold on to the letter until Wednesday before mailing it, in the event I wanted to do any final tuning.

That evening I got a call from Lew Carpenter, who was in Jimmy Orr's restaurant in midtown Atlanta. "What are you doing in town, man?" I asked Lew, surprised to hear his voice.

Lew said he was fed up with Van Brocklin in Minnesota and was on his way to talk with Norb Hecker, head coach of the Falcons. He said he had quit the Viking staff and invited me to come down for a drink. Jimmy's place was a hangout for Atlanta's sports establishment and it was no secret that Lew and I spent the evening in a corner booth engaged in deep conversation.

I told Lew about the letter I was planning to send.

On Wednesday, just after I returned from the post office, I got a call from Al Thomy, a sportswriter for the Atlanta *Constitution*. He asked me if I'd sent a letter to the Vikings' management saying I would not return. I fumbled around for an answer, finally ad-libbing that rumors about my situation were flying everywhere in the pro football business and refusing further comment. The next morning Thomy had a short squib in the *Constitution* making note of the rumored letter. That brought a call from an old friend, Jim Minter, sports editor of the Atlanta *Journal*. Had I sent a letter? He asked.

"Jim, I can't say anything," I pleaded.

That did it. Jim saw that in answer to a direct question, I could not deny the letter. Jim, as a good newspaperman, sensed a story and wrote a strong confirmation of Thomy's piece and put it on the national wires.

At this point the U.S. mail was carrying my letter northward, where it arrived in the Viking office on Friday. Jim Finks and Bernie Ridder called immediately and wanted to get together in Chicago. I told them it was too late for that; that my decision was final and who they wanted to coach their football team was completely up to them. I wanted out, no matter what, and it was too late to make any compromises. About then Minter's wire story reached the Vikings and I learned later that they were furious. To them it looked as if I were trying a power play, a shoot-the-moon effort to get Van Brocklin out of Minnesota. Naturally that was not the case; they should have known that once the matter was made public I could never have returned to the team and expect to be an effective leader. Talk about credibility gaps!

Little did I know that my future was already determined. The Vikings' staff had informed Wellington Mara of the Giants that I was available for trade as early as December, and by the time my letter had arrived, the deal had practically been closed. As I learned later, two starting NFL quarterbacks had been on the block at that time—San Francisco's John Brodie and myself. In one of the biggest wisdom lapses in football history, the 49er front office had decided that John had lost his job to either George Mira or Steve Spurrier and was ready to let him go elsewhere. Fortunately for them, nobody was willing to come up with the right deal and Brodie stayed around to lead San Francisco to their only championship. Spurrier is still on the 49er bench, and Mira has floated around the NFL without finding a permanent home.

Four teams made serious bids for my services. New York was willing to pay the most, followed by Detroit, Chicago and the Pittsburgh Steelers. New York gave a bundle. In the 1967 draft, which was only a few days hence, the Giants agreed to give up their first- and second-round draft choices, plus their bonus number-one choice in 1968 (received as compensation for the New York Jets' franchise encroachment during the AFL-NFL merger agreement), plus a 1969 number-two draft choice. That meant the loss of a bunch of young talent for the Giants, and its effect on the club would be tremendous for a number of seasons; but the irony of the situation was that, as in so many trades and drafts, the results never worked out as anticipated. The number-one draft choice in 1967 brought running back Clinton Jones to the

Vikings. He has never been a consistent starter for the team. The 1968 number-one choice produced Ron Yary, a superb offensive lineman, but players at these positions never dictate the course of a game like a quarterback, a great runner or a middle linebacker. Offensive linemen are rarely drafted first, but in 1968, a thin talent year in the colleges, he was the best available. Ed White, a guard, and Bob Grim, a wide receiver, came from the number-two draft choices. Both occupy the Vikings' bench. The irony is that after all the smoke had settled over my trade, another deal with the Rams later in the year turned out to be tremendously important for the future of Minnesota. In a move that generated very little interest at the time, the Vikings traded Tommy Mason and Hal Bedsole, both of whom had bad knees, to Los Angeles for Marlin McKeever and an intense young lineman named Alan Page. The Vikings then dealt McKeever to Washington for safety Paul Krause. The upshot of the story is this: Anyone in Minnesota will tell you the two men who welded the Viking defense into the magnificent unit it is were none other than Page and Krause.

When I ended my phone conversation with Finks the day my letter had arrived, I figured the great Tarkenton-Van Brocklin struggle was over. But Dutch always had a way of coming up with the last surprise. The following day the world learned that Norm Van Brocklin had quit as a coach of the Vikings. Outside the Viking management, little is known about his departure except that Van Brocklin got a cash settlement on his contract. I've never heard of any football coach having a clause in his contract that granted him a settlement in the event he resigned.

So there it was; in a cataclysmic few hours, the two protagonists in Minnesota's biggest sports feud were gone, Van Brocklin ultimately headed to my hometown in Atlanta as coach of the Falcons, and me to New York, where I was supposed to wallow in riches and fame. Flying into New York for my first meeting with the Giants management and coaching staff, I could only wonder what effect it was going to have on the Giants—an aggregation that I felt was the worst in football. I had a chance to be a hero if I could make them win, or a bum if I couldn't. Either way, I was sure it was going to be some kind of big deal. Much bigger than anything I could have imagined in Minnesota.

III

As I WHEELED into New York as the Great White Hope, my addition to the Giants practically guaranteed them losing seasons for the immediate future. They had spent dearly to get me, and the four major draft choices extracted by the Vikings seemed to remove the possibility that the team would pick up the major talent it needed. It is standard among fans and the press to lay the fortunes of any football team at the feet of two men—the quarterback and the coach. If things are not going well, these guys are the ones who suffer, whose replacement is screeched for and who catch the loudest boos. On the other hand, if the team wins, they are usually the principal heroes. Either way, the situation is crazy. Football teams build dynasties with defense—relentless pass rushers, mobile, hard-nosed linebackers and far-ranging secondary men. No team has won a major championship in professional football without a powerful defense. But many, like the 1963 Bears, the Conerly-era Giants, the '64–'66 Buffalo Bills of the AFL, the 1969 Vikings and even the great Packer teams of Lombardi, often won with offenses that were potent enough only to take advantage of the breaks provided them by the defense.

Its interesting to note that the 1968 New York Jets won the

Super Bowl with a superb defense—a defense so proficient that Joe Namath was able to attempt fewer passes during that season than any other in his career. Take a look at the all-time passing leaders, headed by John Unitas with more than 4,500 passing attempts in fifteen seasons. During that period his Colts won six league titles, a conference championship and split two games in the Super Bowl. Now consider Bart Starr, who ranks third among passers, also with fifteen seasons in the pros. Over that span he and the Packers won five league championships, one conference title and two straight Super Bowls. But Bart has attempted *1,500* fewer passes than Unitas over the same number of years and has gained approximately 14,000 fewer yards!

Sonny Jurgensen ranks second as a passer, with dazzling statistics, but he's never played with a winner. The same goes for myself, down there in fifth place in the all-time lists. In 1967 Sonny set NFL records with 288 passes completed in 508 attempts, gaining a fantastic 3,747 yards. What a milestone, except that the Redskins won only *five* games that season. The same year Namath threw the ball 491 times and gained a record 4,007 yards, but the Jets gave up 329 points to the opposition and won only eight games in a very weak division. Big headliner quarterbacks—the guys with the grace and power to fling a football through a hardwood door at 80 yards—can do almost everything: fill the stadiums and endless columns of newsprint, electrify crowds, set records, make game-busting plays and get carried around the field on the shoulders of adoring teammates; but they cannot single-handedly make a winning football team. That takes a magnificent defense coupled with a balanced offense. Both must rely on a cool, disciplined brand of football featuring sure blocking and tackling coupled with inspired running and cool, ball-control passing. Sure, a quality quarterback is helpful, and a weak man at that position can nullify the efforts of an otherwise solid team, but my point is that no one, from Sammy Baugh to Otto Graham to John Unitas, has ever been able to win solely on the strength of his right arm. And in the end, when it's all written, the question is whether or not you're a winner or loser. That's the bottom line.

When I arrived at little Fairfield College in the summer of 1967, I figured I was joining a Giants team that was collectively the least-talented forty-man outfit in football. There were few guys I could describe as quality football players and a number of them were over the hill. Jim Katcavage, for example, had been a stalwart in the great defenses of the early sixties, but he was nearing retirement. Vince Costello was a jaunty, free-wheeling middle linebacker who'd played on some great Cleveland Brown teams. He'd been cut and been picked up as a stopgap by the Giants and been figured to bring experience and aggressiveness to the club, but the end of his career was in sight. Fortunately, he had one last great year left in that battered, paunchy body of his.

At thirty-two the graceful, sure-handed Del Shofner had lost most of his speed and it was likely that he would make the final catch of a memorable career during the upcoming season. Darrell Dess, a powerful, agile guard who had punched open innumerable holes for the likes of Alex Webster and Phil King during the great years, had returned after being traded but was beginning to show the lumps and scars of endless Sundays in the pit. These men had been winners on proud football teams, and despite their public optimism it was clear to them that they were on their way to retirement hooked to a lightweight club with barely a prayer for another championship.

There was a small nucleus of men in their prime—solid football players who provided the Giants with whatever strength they had. Joe Morrison was short and slow, hardly the kind of player you'd look for to propel an NFL offense. But Joe had the curious ability to do whatever he set out to do, be it squirming through an unyielding line for first-down yardage, speeding downfield to snare a crucial pass or flinging his small body against a defensive lineman to execute a block. Morrison was known throughout the league as one of those guys who could beat a good football team with sheer determination. He was constantly being acclaimed along with Tom Matte of the Colts and Dick Hoak of the Steelers as pro football's counterpart to the utility infielder, but that was hardly his biggest asset to the team. Joe Morrison was a fighter, a money player every minute of the game with that mysterious ability—almost a sixth sense—to find a fleeting hole in the line or a bare patch of grass on a pass pattern and to somehow manhandle the ball closer to the goal line than a man half again his size. The Giants needed Joe Morrison the way the Israelites needed David.

We had three quality offensive linemen. Greg Larson had succeeded Ray Wietecha at center during the championship years and was as good as any in the league. Greg had returned from a critical knee injury in 1964 which had sidelined him in sixty-five—an injury so grievous that the doctors were fearful not that they could not get him back into football, but that they could not fix him well enough so that he would walk without a limp! Pete Case, "Ol' Goober," a teammate of mine at Georgia in 1959, had started as a rookie guard for the Eagles in 1962 and was one of the few on the Giants with all-pro qualifications. A tall, rangy guy whose unabashed sentimentality made him appear on the surface an unlikely candidate for pro football, much less All-Star status. But back in those muggy, uncertain days of spring training, I knew that if we were going to establish any sort of running game at all, it was going to be up to Larson, Case and a stubby, 270-pound tackle named Willie Young. Willie is listed in the program at 6 feet, but he's actually only 5' 10½", making him very nearly as wide as he is tall. However, Willie's great nimbleness and skill as a zone blocker made him a key man in our offensive line. For that kind of contribution to the team, we were even willing to tolerate Willie's awful off-key singing in the shower.

Defensively, we could count on one other man in addition to Vince Costello. At free safety we were fortunate to have Spider Lockhart, an All-Pro player who was (and still is), in my opinion, the best man at that position in the entire league. Spider was simply a superb defensive player, with good speed, vast range and an irrational urge to assault 220-pound running backs and tight ends. The rest of our defense was virtually undistinguished

At tight end we had Aaron Thomas, another Giant who had been around during the great years. Endowed with good speed, Aaron offset an inability to block with vast experience at running pass patterns to become an effective operator at his position. Although another pass receiver named Homer Jones was to gather most of the headlines that year, it was Aaron who led the team, with 51 receptions for 877 yards and 9 touchdowns. But Homer, I think, saved me. Without him we would have had no deep threat, none of the ability to strike quickly that a spotty offense needs so badly. Obviously, ball control is the classic way to win football games, but even Vince Lombardi and Bart Starr couldn't have made it work without a couple of guys like Carroll Dale and Boyd Dowler who could pick off a ball in the next county if necessary. But with a porous defense like ours limited ability to establish a consistent ball-control offense, a blitzkrieg kind of man like Jones became doubly important.

Homer Jones was a raw football talent. When he first came to the Giants he didn't have the vaguest notion about the nuances of catching passes. He knew only this: If he ran down the field and somebody had enough strength to fling the ball near him, he would catch it and run the rest of the way. Actually Homer never did develop much more than that in the way of subtlety. He didn't need to. He was an instinctive pass catcher, with awesome speed and the bonus capability of being able to overpower defensive backs. Homer had floated around the world of football—first with the Houston Oilers, then with the Giants' taxi squad—before being activated in 1964. When I met him in 1967 his age was officially listed as twenty-six, although I am sure, by his own admission, that he was at least two years older than that. In fact, he may have been knocking on thirty even then. Nevertheless, he had lost none of his speed and it was my good fortune that he chose 1967 to put it all together—to really get into the game of football and bring all his considerable talents to bear. He was never one to go flat out all the time. In fact, if he wasn't involved in the play, it was not uncommon for Homer to take a few feckless steps downfield, then return to the huddle. That we could stand, because Homer was paid to catch passes, gain yards and score touchdowns—all of which he did, catching 49 of the first, gaining 1,209 yards of the second (for a stunning 24.7 average) and scoring 14 of the third. If Homer Jones hadn't felt like running in 1967, I don't know where we'd have ended up.

Coupled with Joe Morrison with his multiple skills, we had a pair of tough young backs who showed tremendous potential. Tucker Frederickson, a good-looking, affable kid from Auburn, had been drafted first by the Giants the same year the Jets were getting all the ink by signing Joe Namath. Tucker had been touted as a potential All-Pro before suffer-

ing a series of awful knee injuries that came within a whisker
of putting him out of football. But he was a fine power runner and an even greater blocker and I knew he was on his
way to becoming a premier fullback if he could only get his
knee back in shape. In the meantime we had another youngster, Ernie Koy, who also had imposing power and barely
enough speed to become the Giants' leading ground gainer
that season.

There they were, a handful of guys among dozens of
beefy hopefuls clumping over the scorched grass of the C. W.
Post College practice field. Some of the rest I could not believe, they were so bad. We had 300-pound linemen who
couldn't cross an intersection at a dead run and beat the
light. We had linebackers who were so clumsy they were in
more danger of hurting themselves than anyone else. And
there were guys—just guys in brush cuts and sweat pants—
who looked as if they might have wandered into camp in
hopes of rustling up a game of touch. It was awful. After a
week in camp I sat down in the locker room and cried. I can
recall wiping away the tears and wondering out loud, "What
in the hell am I doing here?"

When I came to New York, it was very chic to describe
what a dummy Allie Sherman was—how he should be a used-
car salesman in Bayonne rather than the steward of New
York's most sacred sports institution. That brand of talk was
a great injustice to Allie because he had done a tremendous
amount for the New York Giants. People had forgotten that
he had been named NFL Coach of the Year twice, once in
his rookie season in 1961 and again the following year. He
was highly respected among his peers around the league as a
football strategist and his devotion to the game was indis-
putable. They talk about Allie's graduating *cum laude* from
Brooklyn College with a psychology degree, then going off

to ride Greasy Neale's Philadelphia Eagle bench for twelve hundred dollars a year. At 5'10", 160 pounds, Allie probably played professional football with less ability than any other player in history. As a reserve quarterback, he played very little but spent hours soaking up Greasy's lifelong knowledge of the game.

Neale knew that Allie would never make it as a player and advised him to enter coaching. With his prodigious intellect and his love of football, he was ideally suited for the work. At twenty-five he took over the minor league Paterson Panthers and led them to a championship. From there he moved to the staff of the New York Giants, operating as a backfield coach for "Stout" Steve Owen. Allie is the man credited with converting the great Charley Conerly from a single-wing tailback to a T-formation quarterback. During those years the Giants were one of the toughest teams in the NFL and Allie's reputation grew. When Owen retired in 1954 he took the head coaching job at Winnipeg in the Canadian League, had solid successes there, and finally returned to New York in 1959 to run the Giants' offense. The man he replaced as offensive coach was Vince Lombardi. Then, in 1961, when Jim Lee Howell retired, Allie was given the head coaching job, but only after the Giants tried hard to get Lombardi to return from Green Bay.

When Allie stepped into the top spot, there was relatively little to change. The Giants had solid offensive and defensive patterns created by Tom Landry and Lombardi, and an impressive lineup of veteran players. The starters changed very little during Sherman's big years from 1961 to 1963, and there's no question that Sherman faced enormous problems in gradually injecting talent into that holdover team from the Howell-Lombardi-Landry days. Very little fresh talent was fed into the system during Allie's first three years. Injuries and age added to his problems. If he had enjoyed better luck in drafting—if Joe Don Looney and Glynn Griffing had played anywhere up to their college potential, for example—or if even one of the trades for men like Huff and Modzelewski had worked out, Sherman might have been able to keep the Giants in contention for a long time. But the roof caved in on him, and a lot of that was just plain bad luck. In fact, a great number of Allie's toughest critics in the later years had given him strong support when he embarked on his 1963 rebuilding program and they started to open fire only when any idiot could see that his trades and drafts hadn't worked out. What's that they say about hindsight being 20-20?

No matter what they say about Sherman, I had tremendous respect and admiration for him right to the end. Yet, despite his vast understanding and love of the game, it was always difficult to view him in the classic context of a football coach. Most of them are florid, thick-necked men with bellies that have broadened appreciably since their playing days, but Allie looked more like an associate professor of business law at NYU.

Sherman taught me a great deal about the technique of being a pro quarterback; more than Van Brocklin by a considerable margin. Norm was a great over-all football strategist. He understood offenses and defenses and had a knack of finding a team's weakness and attacking it successfully. But he had never devoted any time to refining the skills of his quarterbacks. Here was one of the greatest forward passers in NFL history, seventh in the all-time standings, endowed with vast knowledge about the position, but he had never spent any substantial time with me, VanderKelen, Berry or any of the Viking quarterbacks to teach us technique. On the other hand, I came to New York and into the hands of Allie Sherman, a candidate for the worst quarterback in the annals of pro football, and he taught me a great deal! Allie spent hours working on my drop-backs, setups, handoffs—all those little subtleties that contribute to perfect play execution. My expertise as a T-formation quarterback increased considerably during my association with him. In fact, I think that is the single most rewarding thing I gained from my relationship with Allie.

But wait a minute, what's this about me describing myself as a "T-formation" quarterback? After all, I'm supposed to be a "scrambler," whatever that means, and isn't it presumptuous of me to include myself with that elite group of men known as classic T-formation quarterbacks? Maybe so, but this "scrambler" image has gotten tiresome over the years. It's bugged me, no question about it, because it's a classic example of that closed-loop thing where writers and players simply repeat what they've read someplace else. They don't give it any thought and you can't believe how many professional football players rate their rivals solely on what they read in the papers or hear on the radio. It's unbelievable, because this means they're evaluating players through unprofessional eyes. A sportswriter in one town might ask the local team's middle linebacker before a game with the Giants, "What do you think of Tarkenton?" So the guy has been reading the papers and he says, "Of course he's a scrambler, so we'll have to . . . blah, blah." So the next time another sportswriter sits down at the typewriter to write something about me, he'll automatically come up with the scrambler thing and maybe use the aforementioned middle linebacker as a source, when it's possible that neither guy has ever seen me play and has only read about me in the papers! In psychology, they call that a reinforcement syndrome.

I am positive that games have been won and lost on the basis of what players felt about the opposition simply from reading the papers. For example, Dick Butkus of the Bears has this image of being an animal, a Neanderthal man, a killer ape, which is absolutely not true. Dick is one of the smartest defensive players in the game. He is a tough player, although far from the outsized sadist he's made out to be. But I am sure a lot of players have been intimidated, not by Dick himself, but by the reputation they've read about long before they ever saw the man take a step on a football field!

In my case, I am a "scrambler" and that is fried into the brain of every sportswriter in the country. What's more, the cliché says, "scramblers can't win." Of course nobody understands what the term means, and I've asked writers exactly what they thought a scrambler did to separate himself from other quarterbacks. Did he leave the classic passing pocket five times a game? Three times a game? Every time he threw the ball? Nobody has ever been able to give me a sensible answer. Their only impression seems to be that a scrambler has no pattern; that he simply grabs the ball from center, sends everybody except the coaching staff downfield and darts around like a mad rabbit until he finds somebody open. That's nonsense of course, but once you're stuck with the label, that's it; that's the bottom line on your scouting report. As for myself, I think a great deal of the scrambler thing can be attributed to the highlight films of my early years with the Vikings. Naturally the scramble plays were the most spectacular, so they tended to get into the films and reinforced the impression.

Speaking of highlight films, students of the game might be wise to seek out the 1960 Los Angeles Rams highlights film, where the announcer describes their young quarterback Frank Ryan as "the premier scrambler in the National Football League"! Frank Ryan? The dispassionate mathematics professor who guided the Cleveland Browns to the NFL Championship, being described as a scrambler a year before I entered the league? But I thought scramblers couldn't win. Recently I was sitting around with about fifteen New York sportswriters and we got into this thing about "scramblers can't win." I said to them the statement indicates ignorance and inconsistency and asked them if they could recall any scrambler who's ever led an NFL team to a championship.

They automatically answered no.

"Who won the 1969 NFL title?" I asked them.

"The Minnesota Vikings," somebody answered.

"Who was their quarterback?"

"Er, Joe Kapp," somebody said, hesitantly.

"Now what do you call Joe Kapp? He rolled out, he bootlegged, he moved around the backfield, he ran with the ball. Now if you're going to call me a scrambler, are you going to call Joe Kapp a classic drop-back quarterback?"

The point is this: I don't call Joe Kapp a scrambler, nor do I think of myself as a scrambler. Both of us, like a great percentage of our counterparts in pro football, are nothing more than T-formation quarterbacks who move around when they feel there is an offensive advantage to be gained.

But the scrambler thing still hangs on. During a telecast of a 1970 Detroit Lions game, my long-time friend Curt Gowdy made a reference to the running of the Lions' fine young quarterback, Greg Landry (a guy who I think is destined for future greatness in the game). Curt said, "The Lions point out that Greg is not a scrambler; he's a runner." Now what does that mean? During the 1970 season Greg Landry had two games during which he rushed over 100 yards. A fair percentage of that yardage came when his receivers were covered and Greg opted to advance the ball rather than eat it for lost yardage. That makes him a "runner," which is acceptable, rather than a "scrambler," which has some sort of stigma attached.

During the 1970 season I ran 42 times, which is about average for my career in pro ball. Or should I say "scrambled"? Either way, a number of successful quarterbacks have run with the ball. Unitas and Jurgensen do so more than you might think. Roman Gabriel does. Bart Starr does. So does John Brodie. And Otto Graham, who played on more championship teams than any other major quarterback, ran a great deal! In contrast is my old coach Norm Van Brocklin, who coined that aged, overused wheeze, "A quarterback should only run out of sheer fright."

In Dutch's case that was true, because he was very likely the slowest quarterback who ever played the game. It was a farce to watch him waddle down the field, but his arm was one of the greatest ever. Therefore he would have been crazy to try running. But what about a young man with tremendous mobility and speed like Bob Griese of the Miami Dolphins? Again, here's a kid who is said to be all tied up in this scrambler-runner-classic drop-back quarterback idiocy to a point where nobody makes any sense. Again, it was a 1970 televised game, one of ABC's Monday-night shows, and Miami was playing the Atlanta Falcons. Howard Cosell got on the mike and punched out the following words in classic Cosell style: "Dolphins coach Don Shula has done a great job with the young Bob Griese, bringing him along as a premier quarterback in the American Conference. Griese was a scrambler, but now Shula has gotten him to stay within the confines of the pocket."

Maybe so, but that night Griese won the game with two key pass plays, both of which resulted from a pair of the wildest so-called scrambles ever transmitted on the tube! But Cosell was right in a sense, Bob Griese is not a scrambler.

Nor am I. We are both quarterbacks with the speed and mobility to move out of the pocket if the situation so demands. Today it's perfectly acceptable for a Griese or a Landry or a Bradshaw to move around in the backfield, but in 1961 when I came into the league, I must have looked like some kind of lunatic loping around back there, especially in contrast to the established quarterbacks, most of whom were about as mobile as sixteen-inch shore batteries. So I am the only pure "scrambler" in football and I'll live with that image for my entire career. That is supposed to have somehow blunted my effectiveness and I can only make this rebuttal: In the ten years I have played, I have had only a few first-rank receivers to throw to; yet despite playing with an expansion team and a few seasons with a badly crippled Giant club, I've somehow managed to pass for more touchdowns *per season* than any other quarterback in history, while gaining over 20,000 yards and scoring over 200 touchdowns by passing—both of which are milestones enjoyed by only five players in the annals of the game. Therefore, it's difficult for me to believe I could have increased my effectiveness if I'd tried to pass *only* when safely huddled behind a wall of protective linemen.

Ironically, I arrived in the NFL with a reputation for being a pretty good passer but an average college runner. My immediate predecessor at Georgia, Charley Britt, was considered way ahead of me as a running quarterback and I came to the Vikings prepared to operate a conventional passing attack. But George Shaw played quarterback during that first exhibition season and our novice offensive line was hardly equipped to keep the veterans off George's back. To make matters worse, George was suffering from a serious knee injury and he simply didn't have the mobility to move around and protect himself. When I finally got a chance to play, I swore I wasn't going to settle for that business of eating the ball. If my protection broke down, I was going to do *something*—to make yardage, dammit, which is what an offense is supposed to do—rather than flop helplessly on the ball. I got the starting quarterback's job in part by doing this, and it worked. Operating in the rugged Western Conference of the NFL, the Vikings won three games that year, in contrast to the Dallas Cowboys, who came into the weaker Eastern Conference a year earlier and went 0-11-1. What's more, I tied a rookie record by throwing 18 touchdown passes, so we must have been doing something right.

This should be added: During all my years with the Vikings, playing under Dutch Van Brocklin, the prototype "tower of strength" drop-back quarterback, he never once told me *not* to run with the football.

Images can be deceiving. And that's one of the major reasons I don't read the newspapers during the football season. I figure, if those guys can be so wrong about me, how can they be correct about anybody else? Football, like anything done in front of the public, is partly an ego trip and I admit I used to love to read all that good stuff the guys were pounding out about my career. But I hated to read the bad things about the poor games, the criticism. That's true with all the players, and any guy in football who says criticism in the press doesn't bother him is either a liar or very adept at kidding himself. So, I decided not to read the papers. Then I wouldn't be effected pro or con; I couldn't get too impressed with myself after the good days or too depressed after the bad. So far that's worked just fine.

Not only did I come to New York with this iron-clad image of a scrambler, but the press had somehow decided that I was some kind of Billy Graham in shoulder pads, a pigskin Elmer Gantry. The standard cliché lead for a story about me might read, "Fran Tarkenton, the pious, hymn-singing southern preacher's son who scrambles his way to glory on the grid-iron . . ." Oh, wow. I don't really care for labels, but in the case of my religious beliefs I have been labeled and put in a box. Sure, I am the son of a preacher and had an extremely strong fundamentalist background during my formative years. I was deeply involved in the Fellowship of Christian Athletes and spent a great deal of time talking with church groups about what I thought to be a proper Christian way of life.

As I matured I saw that in order to grow intellectually and spiritually I had to have a basis for what I believed. To do that, I was forced to re-examine many things I never questioned in my youth. I remain convinced of the basic good of the Church, but I have become aware of its shortcomings. The essential mission of the Church must relate to people—all people, in the ghetto as well as the suburb.

Tarkenton Ventures, my Atlanta business, is a genuine extension of these instincts. We are specialists in teaching such basic skills as reading and writing to the underprivileged and quite frankly I believe that if I can help to improve the lot of one man—to teach him to read and aid him in getting a job and achieving some sense of pride and accomplishment—I have made as strong a religious gesture as I can.

Like my scrambler image, I have been labeled as something of a religious prude. Nothing is further from the truth. I have increasingly broadened my understanding about the entire scope of social habits and I think I express myself in these areas with a naturalness and freedom that simply doesn't dovetail with my public portrait. My religion is much closer to that of the more progressive church leaders these days than to the old ways. *Jesus Christ, Superstar* says a great deal more to me personally than many of the conventional hymns.

IV

PRIOR TO THE OPENING of the 1969 Giants' training camp, Allie Sherman said to me, "Somehow, we've got to get rid of this seven-and-seven syndrome we've been operating in."

He was referring to the Giants' having finished at .500 in the two previous seasons and somehow implied that a little more effort, a little more desire, a little more sacrifice, were all we needed to turn the team into a winner. "Wait a minute, Allie," I retorted, "you know and I know the only way we're going to make headway is to get *people* in here. We need talent; the team is just plain lacking the horses, and all the planning and pep talk in the world isn't going to make up for that." In fact, we had been lucky to win seven games each in sixty-seven and sixty-eight. We weren't even that good, if the truth be known. I know we beat teams that were better than we were, and what's more, *they* knew they were better than we were! Somehow, thanks to Homer Jones and Vince Costello and Aaron Thomas and Spider Lockhart and a few others, we stumbled and lucky-bounced as far as we got. But the New York Giant fans demand winners and they had experienced five seasons in a row in which their best had been mediocre and their worst had been record shattering.

58

We started out in 1968 by doing better than we expected. Somehow we won our first four games, which boosted everybody's hopes to improbable altitudes. We were heading for a fall. Just before the end of the half of our fifth game, against Atlanta, I separated my right shoulder. We lost that one by a single point. They pumped my arm full of everything except lead-free Amoco during the next week trying to make emergency repairs for the San Francisco 49ers. I didn't throw a ball until the morning of the game and not really effectively again for the rest of the season. We lost to San Francisco. Then, improbably, we struggled back to a point where we headed into our last three games with a 7–4 record and giddy hopes of a high finish in our division. We played the mighty Los Angeles Rams dead even for fifty-nine minutes. With seconds remaining we tied the score 21–21, then watched helplessly while the Rams clumped back down the field and scored a field goal to beat us 24–21. Another pair of losses to Cleveland and St. Louis and there we were at seven-and-seven again—which may be a pretty good cocktail but is a lousy record in the NFL—any way you mix it.

Sherman's time was running out and he knew it. Fortunately, we'd finally gotten a chance to make a first-round draft choice again and had picked a long-haired, free-spirited defensive end off the California beaches named Fred Dryer. He had all the equipment to be one of the finest pass rushers in football, and for the first time since I'd arrived with the Giants, we could look forward to having an absolutely top-quality rookie in camp. Freddie rolled into town looking more like an outsized surfer than a professional football player. That caused some trouble. Long hair and freaky clothes were simply not part of the Giant image in those days and younger players like Dryer were not understood. The self-image of the perfect Giant was a cool, well-mannered gentleman with close-cropped hair and a Brooks Brothers suit whose briefcase was packed with football plays and bond quotations. Horn-rimmed glasses were optional.

But times were changing and the Giants organization seemed to be gathering itself together for one final pitched battle against reality. Across town the Jets had developed into a relaxed gang of individuals, operating with every life-style from the far-out to the conservative, while great pressure was building for us to function like a group of the stuffiest Princeton alumni you can imagine. This "image" had been prevalent with the Giants for a long time and I can remember when, just after coming to the team, I was confronted by a veteran who said, "You can stay with this team a long time if you just keep your mouth shut and don't make trouble." Other suggestions in the same vein had been voiced and I found it curious that while there was plenty of talk about style, there was very little talk about winning. Ironically, the great Giant teams had been led by strong, spirited individuals like Gifford, Rote and Webster, who refused to conform to any specific team image but had a tremendous urge to win.

A new generation of football players like Fred Dryer, coupled with the apparently successful freedom of expression within the Jets (after all, they'd just won the Super Bowl) and the mounting pressure to produce a winner, influenced Allie to move backward, not forward. He seemed to have decided that a reversion to the foreign legion tactics of Lombardi—which may have worked in 1960 but not in 1969— would magically reinforce all that hoary Giant tradition and somehow weld us into a single-minded, brush-cut army of winners. Instead of loosening up in the face of the new trends, Allie reacted to them and turned himself into something he could not be. Allie Sherman was too nice a guy to be a martinet.

Just before practice opened in 1969, Allie said to me, "Success this year depends on two things—our defensive line and what kind of season you have. In fact, we've got the defensive line about straightened out, so it boils down to you."

"What do you mean by that, Allie?" I asked, hardly concealing my irritation. "My shoulder is fine and I'm a proven product, a veteran with a consistent record, so you know what I'm going to do, but how can you be so sure about the front four? What have you done to change things there? The best front four in our conference belongs to Dallas and they've got guys like Bob Lilly, Jethro Pugh and George Andrie. What do you think you've got to match them?"

"Well, we've got a new pass rusher coming in," he said bravely.

"Who's that?" I asked, my hopes rising.

"Joe Szczecko."

"*Joe Szczecko?*" I asked in a mild state of shock. "You mean the Joe Szczecko who's only five nine and weighs two-forty, the guy Atlanta put on waivers? Joe's a great boy, but you're going to put him up against Lilly and Pugh and those guys? Come on, Allie, be serious."

"Yeah, but we got this kid Vernon Vanoy and there's Dryer and we'll just put 'em in there with Lurtsema and Joe and let 'em *go!*"

"Go where? You can't expect a defensive line like that to stack up in this league!"

"But we've got a new line coach, Jim Trimble. I had my doubts about Jack Patera, and Trimble will do the job," he said.

"Doubts? Doubts about Jack Patera?" I asked, wondering if I was losing my mind. "But, Allie, Jack is the guy who developed the Rams' Fearsome Foursome." (Little did I know that he was on the way to the Vikings, where he would turn the Purple Gang—Eller, Marshall, Page and Larsen—into another legend.) "He's got to be one of the best line coaches in the game."

"You wait and see," Sherman said tartly. "We'll take care of the front four. You just worry about yourself."

After that conversation, I knew we were in deep trouble.

His training camp that year was the most depressing football scene I've ever witnessed and I felt terribly sorry for the man. He was in a box and he was pressing to get out. The harder he tried to organize things, the more chaotic they became. The tougher he got with the players, the more they withdrew. I've never seen an unhappier, worse-motivated collection of football players in my life. Not only was Sherman losing control of his team, but he was catching increasing flak from the press and, maybe most important of all, the retired Giants. They felt that they had been treated badly by Sherman and that he had been responsible for the disintegration of the proud dynasty they had created. These older guys had a powerful influence on the active players, which further eroded the coach's ability to control the team.

We staggered out of camp to play our traditional exhibition opening with Green Bay. Our minds weren't on the game (which we lost) for a number of reasons, the most important of which was the upcoming encounter with the Jets. Our first confrontation with the new boys from Shea Stadium—the guys who had taken over part of *our* town and had made us look inept in the process—was played for blood. Mostly ours, as it turned out. The game was set for the Yale Bowl and it was a sellout. Sherman and the coaches had been working on a game plan for most of the winter and that had added even more pressure to Allie's troubled mind. If somehow we could dump the Jets, the Cinderellas of the Super Bowl, there was a chance we could march into the regular season on an upbeat. To lose would only shove us farther into despair.

Work as we did, we arrived in New Haven on that muggy Sunday in August, 1969, as probably the worst-prepared team in pro football. The coaches had installed the running game on the previous Monday, then found it didn't work on Tuesday. It was changed again. Then Saturday morning, less than twenty-four hours before the kickoff, Allie announced that he was going to start Joe Morrison at flanker and Aaron Thomas at tight end. Neither man had played at those positions during the entire training camp! Freeman White had expected to be the starting tight end and Joe had been working at halfback and Aaron at flanker, but suddenly that was all changed, with Sherman reasoning that a "veteran" lineup like this would be more effective, at least for the opening series of downs. What's more, he said we "owed" a starting assignment to Aaron and Joe. We never altered that lineup once the game started. On the other hand, Bob Lurtsema, a tower of strength on the lean years' defensive lines, was scheduled to ride the bench in favor of Tim McCann, a rookie from Princeton.

The score could have been 100 to nothing. Here we were, in a state of near-chaos, going up against the Jets in their absolute prime. They started their veterans and they played them until the game was about out of reach—which took about seventeen minutes if my memory serves me correctly, when the score reached 28–0. I can remember five instances in the game in which we fielded ten men; another when we only had nine. Believe me, we were undermanned enough without spotting them a numerical advantage as well. The whole thing was a disaster and the embarrassment drove the Giants deeper into our emotional hole.

Allie kept pushing, which stretched whatever fiber the team had left to the breaking point. We lost two more exhibition games, which under normal circumstances wouldn't have meant anything, but this team was starved for some sense of accomplishment, some collective feeling of self, that could be best expressed by a victory. Constant rumors about Allie's replacement swept through the team.

We had one more try before the regular season opened against the Minnesota Vikings. Our opponents were the Steelers, who were in the same doormat category as we were, and our chances of salvaging at least one exhibition victory seemed bright. The game was to be played in the relative privacy of Montreal, Quebec, and maybe, just maybe, if we could put it all together the gloomy memories of the training camp and the exhibition season could be erased. Allie was thinking about the future. We sat around in his hotel room the afternoon of the game and discussed the possible use of the shotgun formation against the Vikings. He noted that Len Dawson and the Kansas City Chiefs had recently used it with success against the Rams, and speculated we might be able to sting the Vikings, especially in long-yardage situations. It made sense to me and we chatted about it for quite a while. Despite the troubles with the team, Allie and I still worked well together. I liked him. But the box he was in seemed to be getting smaller by the minute.

I was about to leave when his mood changed to pensive and he said quietly and deliberately, "I just don't know what's going to happen. There's a lot of pressure being put on a lot of people."

The Steelers beat us to a chorus of "Good-bye, Allie," sung for the first time in French. We spotted them a substantial lead, then got a rally started in the last quarter which fell short. (What a terrible night that was. There were no more than a few thousand people scattered around the stadium, and I can recall at one point early in the first quarter I was tackled by John Campbell, a Steelers linebacker. As we stood up, John looked at the stands and cracked, "Wow, Tarkenton, you really pack 'em in.") We'd blown our wad and walked off the field and into the dank, shabby dressing room with the catcalls ringing in our ears and our fifth straight defeat pressing on our minds. We were one miserable football team and something was ready to break. Bob Lurtsema started it, accidentally. He stood up on a bench and tried to say something, but the murmur of grumbling players, the thump of sweaty pads and muddy shoes against the concrete floor and the hiss of the nearby showers made it difficult even for a big guy like Bob to be heard. Suddenly something triggered inside me and I jumped up, yelling, "Everybody out of here, everybody out except football players!"

As always, the room was full of guys close to the Giants—friends of the owners, Tim and Wellington Mara, Father Dudley, the team chaplain, and a few other Catholic priests, press aides, equipment managers, trainers, etc. A couple of them heeded my shout and wandered toward the door. Most of them ignored me. "Out, dammit, this is for the players only!" I yelled again and then other players began to pick up my message and started to herd everybody without a uniform toward the exit. This had never happened in a Giants locker room before and there was some complaining as the cadre of team supporters were eased out, but a sense of purpose was spreading across the room and none of them were particularly willing to argue with a gang of guys who were as sore and frustrated as we were.

I don't think I've ever been more emotional in my life.

"This team has been too hung on image," I said stridently. "We're going around worrying about the length of our sideburns or if our clothes are too wild or if somebody will hear us swearing in the dressing room, while the only damned thing we ought to be worrying about is *winning!* We're a bunch of individuals—we're men, for God's sake—we ought to be able to figure out our own life-styles without thinking first how it will fit into some idiotic image. The only thing that counts in the end is how you produce, whether or not you perform on the football field. I don't care if you want to get drunk and go down to Forty-second and Broadway and chase hookers, just as long as you can produce on Sunday! We've got to be ourselves and it's high time we realized it. I want us all to promise ourselves that from here on in the only thing this football team is going to worry about is winning!"

A few other players took up where I left off and before long the session had turned into a great catharsis that we all knew had loosened the team and just might make us more effective on the football field.

I told Allie about the session later that night and he was pleased. He too was at the end of his wits and was convinced that any release of pressure on the players could do nothing but good. We all flew back to New York feeling better than we had in weeks. The next afternoon Tucker Frederickson, Bobby Duhon, Ernie Koy and Tommy Crutcher were having dinner with Elaine and me at our home in Greenwich, Connecticut. Just before dessert was served a phone call told us Allie Sherman had been fired as coach of the Giants.

V

WE WERE STILL staggering around, trying to absorb the news of Allie Sherman's firing, when word was passed hours later that Alex Webster had been named to replace him. Alex the coach? Sure, "Big Red" was in the Giant pantheon of former stars, sure, his head-down assaults as the Giant fullback made him one of the most respected short-yardage runners in football, but Alex was the most junior coach on the team's staff; in charge of the backfield and seemingly overshadowed by a number of other men both in terms of seniority and knowledge of the game. At first it didn't make any sense. But his selection, which I think was made on the basis of pure intuition by Wellington Mara, turned out to be a brilliant move.

Monday's papers were full of the Sherman-Webster switch and how the great Montreal "revolt" had trigged the entire situation. A number of writers, operating with a smattering of rumor, hearsay and conjecture, had decided that our meeting after the Pittsburgh game had been a player rebellion designed to force Sherman out of his job. That was nonsense. Nothing could have been farther from the truth. In fact, Sherman's name had not been mentioned. Our concern had been ourselves—how we were operating as a team. We were groping to get ourselves together. We knew that a great deal of the problem was our own fault, that we simply weren't playing very well. We weren't under any circumstances trying to pass the buck or to make Sherman into the scapegoat. Nevertheless, with less than a week left before we opened the season against the Minnesota Vikings, the press fascinated itself and its readers with details of the great revolution which presumably had resulted in the disposal of Sherman and the improbable elevation of Alex Webster to head coach.

It was a tough time for all of us. A lot of people, on and off the team, found it difficult to believe that Alex had been named to the job. A few hours after his appointment, Alex phoned Roosevelt Brown, the line coach, and announced, "Hey, Rosie, guess what? I'm the new head coach."

"Come on Alex, you've gotta be kidding," replied Rosie. Alex never did convince Brown that he was serious, and Rosie finally called the Giants' office to get official confirmation.

Sherman was suddenly gone, wiped out of our minds as if he'd never existed. That's a sad part of big league sports (although not much different, I suppose, from conventional business), where a guy will be a close comrade-in-arms one day and gone the next. It's a tough sport and every man lives with the reality that if he is unable to produce, he will be replaced. Nothing personal, no hard feelings, just gone. I was sorry to see Allie go but at the same time realized that a natural, easygoing, emotional guy like Alex might be the ideal anecdote for an up-tight collection of players like us. Often when a coach is relieved under such circumstances, it produces an instantaneous upturn in spirits, as if all the foulups, miscues and ineptness had been magically swept out the door with the old regime. That happened, predictably with Alex.

We gave him a standing ovation when he appeared for our first practice session on Tuesday morning. He stood in front of us, the same guy with the bull neck and the proud, pointed jaw and the piercing eyes who had buckled the knees of so many defensive linemen, and said, "Listen, you guys, you know me and you know what kind of a guy I am. I'm not going to change and I'm going to depend on you guys helping me with your suggestions to help put the Giants back where we belong. I think football should be fun and I want it to be fun for you. We can make it fun by working together."

It was just what we needed. Alex's naturalness and *comaraderie* with the team was in perfect contrast to Sherman's strained drill instructor tactics he had tried late in the waning days of his tenure. Our spirits made the magical upturn and we poured onto the field for the Vikings game convinced that we were unbeatable. We were, for a short time. In what was to turn out to be one of the great upsets of the 1969 season we took on the Vikings at Yankee Stadium, got a few providential bounces of the football and some inspired play from everybody and walked off with a 24–23 victory. From that point on the Vikings were to win twelve consecutives games before they lost to Atlanta— coached by another of their alumnus, Norm Van Brocklin.

We were undefeated. For one week. Detroit shut us out 24–0 the following Sunday. Then we squeezed by Chicago 28–24 and wrestled a 10–7 win out of Pittsburgh. We were an amazing 3–1 and we felt a rising optimism about our chances of putting together our first winning season since 1963. Then we blew the next one against Washington 20–14, and Dallas gave us a sound thrashing, 25–3. The emotional high that had existed since Alex's advancement to head coach was col- lapsing amid the successive poundings in our weekly warfare and it was no longer enough to operate on passion alone. We needed some strategic changes, especially on offense. Our last three games had produced a modest 27 points, and Alex was convinced that our ancient but honorable NFL-patented offense was ready for retirement. After all, we'd been using it since the days of Jim Lee Howell and Vince Lombardi. Alex was beginning to evidence a strongly inventive football mind and after talking openly with the veteran members of the team and other coaches, he made the decisions to scrap our offense. I think Alex's greatest strength lay in his insistence upon being himself. So many coaches have failed because they have tried to pattern themselves after another man. Vince Lombardi has been the prototype for a number of professional and college coaches—who have failed simply because they were not Vince Lombardi. The same is true of those who sought to emulate Bear Bryant, Paul Brown and so many others. Alex Webster remained Alex Webster, and after he had solicited opinions he sat down alone and reached the decision to make the big change.

We were known around the league as a standard Red and Brown team. This described us on the basis of the two simple offensive sets we used—and had used for what seemed like the last century. The Red formation split the two running backs behind the offensive tackles; the Brown placed the fullback directly behind the quarterback. That, coupled with the standard use of the flanker and split end, comprised our offense. Nothing terribly complicated about it, but it was the system that Lombardi had taken to Green Bay and with men like Jim Taylor and Paul Hornung running behind the flawless blocking of Forrest Gregg, Fuzzy Thurston, and Jerry Kramer, etc., it had worked to perfection. Tom Landry had exported the system to Dallas, and Bill Austin, another assistant Giant coach, had taken it to the Pittsburgh Steelers. Norb Hecker, a Lombardi assistant at Green Bay, started the

Atlanta Falcons in the NFL with the Red and Brown formation. It was hardly deceptive, to say the least, and without powerful personnel who could execute with the kind of sledgehammer perfection demanded by Lombardi, a team using it was in a great deal of trouble. Landry and others were switching to more sophisticated "multiple" offenses, and Alex decided it was time for us to make the big switch. He announced the move after the Dallas game, and that week was spent experimenting with new sets that included triple flankers, the double wing, the I-formation, the stacked-I, men in motion and quarterback sprint-out passing patterns that permitted me to exploit my mobility (or if you feel more comfortable with clichés, scrambling). It was all very exciting but extremely difficult. The ideal time to make changes of this magnitude is during the cold winter months prior to training camp, not in the middle of a rugged season, witnessed by a legion of fans who are starved for success.

We made a modest introduction of the new system the next week against the Eagles in front of the home crowd in Yankee Stadium. The few new plays we tried seemed to work, but we lost 23–20 amid a rising tide of boos. Then St. Louis bombed us 42–17, but we persisted with the new offense. A major problem involved terminology—that of quickly describing the play in the huddle. We have a mere thirty seconds between plays, and the more time that is consumed calling the play, the less time there is left at the line of scrimmage to examine the defense and make the appropriate adjustments. Split seconds are critical, and the elimination of a single word in a play call can be critical. At that point we simply hadn't developed a new terminology to go with our new offense and I was forced to resort to play calling like "Red right, X and wing square out at five yards, B hold block, A strong side motion." A year later, with our system more highly developed, the same play could be called simply, "Red right 81 pass, A motion." But it was a terribly hard time for us, finding the right terminology for the plays and then executing them properly. I had to spell out, in time-consuming verbiage, exactly which side the halfback would go into motion toward, until we finally decided that the word "motion" would send him sprinting to the strong side and "peel" would put him in motion to the weak side. Backs and pass receivers were given numerical and lettered designations that gave them specific assignments on each play without my having to explain. (We'll examine that in detail later.) It all sounds terribly elementary in retrospect, but the development of a totally new offensive setup, including a number of complicated alignments, had to be perfected step by step, with new blocking assignments, new pass patterns, new backfield formations and new signals all being dovetailed together in the hubbub and confusion of the midseason.

It was the worst six weeks I have ever spent in football. While I could see that the change was leading us somewhere, loss piled on loss—seven of them in seven Sundays—and the confusion and criticism and frustration were about all we could bear. Thankfully there was only one other game in that nightmare—a 25–24 defeat at the hands of lightly regarded New Orleans Saints. The Giants' fans about booed us out of the stadium. They were on me in particular. Heinrich Himmler would have gotten a better reception. It is perfectly natural for the quarterback to catch hell when things go wrong. It is only justifiable considering the adulation we receive when things go right. In fact, I don't really mind the booing, because it shows that the crowd is involved, that it cares about what is going on. When we perform well, they cheer, and when we foul up, they let us know too. By the time we lost our seventh consecutive game all of us on the team felt like booing too, believe me. It's different from college, where the hometown heroes get used to operating in two conditions—deafening cheers or cryptlike silence. College crowds seldom boo their own team. When they are doing badly, the rooters just slump back in their seats and watch the proceedings in a dazed funk. But that is not true in the pros, where the crowds figure they're paying to watch people play the game of football with reasonable competence and when that is not the case they figure they're not getting their money's worth. Bad play equals bad value. They boo.

The local papers didn't help a whole lot either. Although I reinforced my rule about not paying any attention to the press, the critics were getting to the team. Football players in general respond to the press and in this case an air of depression settled over the club. We tried harder with the new offensive system, while the defensive team, though undermanned at linebacker, tried to organize around veterans like Bob Lurtsema and Spider Lockhart and rookie Fred Dryer, who was surpassing all expectations. Through it all Alex kept his cool. Considering his record as a fullback, this was a bit surprising. "Big Red" had been a football player with a temper that tended to go off like a nickel rocket, and with game after game slipping away from us, most of us expected a gigantic blowup. But Alex just paced the sidelines, puffing away on king-size cigarettes and looking worried. In the intervening practice days, we stuck with the new stuff, working to perfect at least part of the system before the season ended.

I'm not sure we would have made it without Joe Morrison. The new offense was perfectly suited to a smart football player like Joe. Playing at halfback, Joe began to run the motion series as well as any man in the game has ever run it, in my opinion. Joe would glide out of the backfield on motion plays and find himself able to read the defensive reactions as if he'd had their playbook tucked under his shirt. Time and again he'd scuttle free and make a key reception. Even if he was covered, he would return to the huddle or sidelines to offer invaluable advice about how to crack the defense the next time. He was to end the season as the team's leading ground gainer (387 yards) and the number-one pass receiver (44 catches for 647 yards and 7 touchdowns). Slowly, in the course of those agonizing weeks, we made subtle adjustments on the basis of what he had seen the linebackers or corner-backs do in a given situation. With four games left, Green Bay stopped us 20–10, but our offense was beginning to make yardage and hope was building. We knew that before the 1969 season was completed somebody was going to get stung by the New York Giants.

We returned home for the second game against St. Louis and when we broke out of the runway and onto the soggy turf of the stadium, I felt like one of the Christians being prodded into the Coliseum. They greeted us with a Bronx cheer they'd been saving up since the New Orleans game.

We deserved it. At that point we were a dazzling three-and-eight on the year and we were about to square off against a team that had beaten us 42–17 only a month earlier. Our fans didn't realize that each week since then the offense had gained some poise and some power. We had been able to move the ball, which of course took some of the load off the defensive team, and we were sure that the Cardinals weren't going to beat us by any 25–point margin this time around. They didn't even come close. The first half was beautiful. It all came together for the first time. The I-formation produced big yardage up the middle, while time and again Morrison swung out oft the backfield to punish them with receptions. The half ended with us holding at 21-point lead.

As we sprinted for the dressing rooms the crowd in Yankee Stadium, still nursing irritated larynxes from weeks of booing, rose to their feet and gave us a standing ovation. I can remember saying to myself as I ducked into the runway and away from the noise, "Man, that's *class*."

This was the beginning. By the time the Cardinals slogged off the field that afternoon we had mauled them worse than any team that had faced the Giants in five years. The final score was 49–6 and we reveled in every last point.

Pittsburgh fell next, amid a thick snowstorm and a muddy field. But the conditions weren't bad enough to keep us from scoring three touchdowns and we slid past them 21–17. We returned to Yankee Stadium for the final game of the season, thinking about some of the back payment we owed the Cleveland Browns. Since the wondrous days of the early sixties, the Browns had viewed us as a pleasant break in the schedule, looking forward especially to the annual trip to New York in the home-and-home series as a weekend of revelry coupled with a light workout on Sunday afternoon. Enough of that. The Browns had been forced to work for their earlier 28–17 win in Cleveland and were sporting a fat 10–2–1 record when they arrived in New York. They left, rather bruised, at 10–3–1. The offense was working even though a number of our best guys had been injured. Don Herrmann and Aaron Thomas, two of our top pass receivers, had been hurt, as had fullbacks Junior Coffey and Tucker Frederickson. Homer Jones, whose speed afoot seemed to be waning rapidly, had filled in at tight end before giving way to second-stringer Butch Wilson. Rich Houston, another reserve, filled in at split end, and Freeman White gave yeoman service at flanker. Despite this patchwork of personnel the multiple formations

—the Giants' New Look—baffled the Browns (who the following week were to dump the Dallas Cowboys for the Eastern Conference Championship) and we won easily 28–17. The season was over and we had weathered the nightmare in the middle to salvage a 6–8 record. Hardly a source of jubilation on the surface, but we left for home with more hope for 1970 than at any other time since I'd been traded to New York. Those last three weeks were all we could remember.

For Alex it was just beginning. He knew we had the basis of a new offense, which would be developed in the 1970 training camp, but he needed bodies most—strong, bright men who could beef up the defense and add consistent zing to the offense. In retrospect we had holes everywhere. It's a wonder we won even six games when I look back at the general level of talent we had on that team. But Alex, operating in concert with Wellington Mara, was becoming extremely aggressive about rooting up some new football players.

He had a little luck. He began inauspiciously enough by obtaining defensive end John Baker from the Canadian League. John was not destined to become a starter for us, but he was a competent, experienced professional football player and his presence added to the depth that we had been lacking for so many years. While we still were without our second-, third- and fourth-round drafts owing to previous deals around the league, we had our first-round choice for the second consecutive year and again the trade paid off. Jim Files, an All-American lineman, came to us from Oklahoma and immediately qualified as one of the potentially great middle linebackers in football. At 6′ 5″, 245, with impressive mobility and a particularly adept mind for football, Jim is on his way to All-Pro status with a few more years of seasoning. A deal with the Detroit Lions in the fourth round produced UCLA's Wesley Grant, another first-class defensive lineman. Until an injury in the exhibition schedule knocked him out for the entire regular season, Wesley was set to play defensive end, making him, with Files, the only other rookie to be included in the starting lineup. Our ninth-round choice was Pat Hughes from Boston University, who was to make the team as backup center for Greg Larson but proved both his worth as a plucky member of the special teams and his potential as a future linebacker. Therefore we gathered up three players in the early rounds of the draft and they all made the team; one started, one would have had he not been hurt and the third was a key reserve. To find this kind of talent in any draft is a dream of every team in football, but to the Giants, starved as they had been in previous drafts, it seemed like some outlandish fantasy come true.

But if that was providential, the Cleveland trade seemed to stretch our good fortune to the limit. The entire deal transpired during those frantic days of the draft and materialized out of Cleveland's desperate search for a young quarterback to back up Bill Nelsen. Bill had been laboring for the Browns with what were widely known as the most damaged knees in football. It seemed at times as if only personal courage kept Bill propped up, and the Cleveland management knew he might end his career if he bumped against his living room coffee table the wrong way. Two quality quarterbacks, Terry Bradshaw and Mike Phipps, had come out of the colleges, and the Browns were hot on the trail of one or the other. Phipps, who had gone to Miami in the first round, seemed most available. The Dolphins had Bob Griese, who is one of the best in the business, and they were willing to barter Phipps for a frontline deep receiver to complement Griese's powerful arm. If Cleveland wanted Phipps, they said, it would cost them Paul Warfield—surely one of the most grace-ful, deceptive and sure-handed deep receivers in the game. The Browns' management, realizing Paul was one of the most popular members of their team, barricaded the office doors in expectation of riots on the part of their public, gulped hard and made the deal. That left them with two things—a multitude of furious fans and a roster lacking a deep receiver. Although Homer Jones had caught 42 balls for 744 yards the previous season, he had been replaced in the starting lineup during our final surge and we knew he was slowing down. What's more, our new offense required that all the receivers run carefully planned patterns on each passing play—something Homer undertook with less than complete enthusiasm. Homer seldom ran full bore unless he was sure the ball was coming to him, and his privately ad-mitted thirty-two years were gnawing away at his blazing speed. I knew this for a fact, because I had been forced to let up slightly on my long passes to Homer in 1969, whereas in the previous two years he could reach anything I had the strength to throw. Homer Jones became expendable.

On the surface I suppose Homer looked great to the Browns. He seemed to be the kind of game breaker they needed to replace Warfield. Ron Johnson had opened the 1969 season in place of the injured LeRoy Kelly and in his debut in the NFL had gained over 100 yards. But it's impossible to keep a man like Kelly on the bench and once he healed, Ron Johnson saw spotty duty for the rest of the year. Bo Scott, a bruising, durable Canadian League veteran with strength up the middle took the other running back position, and Johnson, who is a near duplicate of Kelly (outside speed, strength, maneuverability, great instincts and impressive pass-catching ability), became a reserve. A running back can do a lot worse than resemble LeRoy Kelly, and Ron Johnson seemed to be an ideal halfback for the new Giant offense.

It seems reasonable that a straight trade, Ron Johnson for Homer Jones, would have been made, but Wellington Mara exhibited inspired skill as a trader. Somehow he managed to convince Cleveland that Homer Jones was such a dynamite performer that they would have to give up more than Johnson. Miraculously the Browns obliged by tossing in Jim Kanicki, a defensive tackle with seven years' experience, and Wayne Maylen, a reserve middle linebacker. Kanicki had a reputation as being abundantly talented but given to lapses when he did not perform at full power. What's more, he was recovering from a broken leg, and the presence of rookie Jerry Sherk gave Cleveland confidence that he could be replaced.

Therefore Cleveland thought they were giving up three reserves for one starter. But the way it turned out, they gave up two starters—Johnson, a 1,000-yard ground gainer, and Kanicki, a defensive stalwart—for one reserve. Homer was beaten out of his job by a two-year man named Fair Hooker (who my old buddy Don Meredith insists has the greatest name in football) and was relegated to kickoff returns and other odd jobs. It is, in my opinion, the greatest, most accidentally lopsided trade in my memory and it literally thrust the Giants into a new era.

While the big news of that drafting session centered around the Johnson-Jones business, Alex made another deal that was to loom as one of the most important negotiations we made all year. We granted Atlanta, through a roundabout deal with Philadelphia, a fifth-round draft choice for a stubby, hard-driving defensive tackle named Jerry Shay. A five-year veteran, Jerry had been drafted number one by the Vikings while I'd still been there, and I can recall being impressed with the kid's gutty play. But he'd been released by the Vikings for some reason or another and after I'd failed to convince the Giants to give him a try, he'd picked up with the Falcons for two seasons. I'd talked with a number of offensive centers and guards around the league and they'd confirmed that Shay was an imposing man to face for a full game. He was not known for his speed or size (he was only 6' 2", 245, which is modest-sized for an interior defensive lineman), but his relentless style of play—his ability to play competitive, consistent football for game after game without letup—was reminiscent of a man like Dick Modzelewski, and Jerry was destined to produce mightily for the Giants all year.

Alex had talked Y. A. Tittle into giving us some pre-season coaching and general counsel, and out of this came two more Giant starters. Y. A. knew we as well as Cleveland were in the market for a deep receiver, and he knew just the man for the job. The San Francisco 49ers were prepared to trade Clifton McNeil, a willowy, easy-running guy who'd led the league in pass receptions two years earlier. I understand San Francisco felt that Clifton was reluctant to run with the ball once he caught it and was too eager to seek refuge at the sidelines. At the same time ol' Clifton weighed only 187 pounds and it seemed to me he was doing his duty simply if he could penetrate the enemy secondary and catch the ball. In any case, we traded my old pal Tommy Crutcher, who was one of the best-liked guys on the team, to Los Angeles for some low-draft choices, which we in turn dealt to San Francisco for McNeil. Tommy was expendable because of a serious knee injury, and while we were all sorry to separate, he knew and we knew that a professional football player learns early in the game to build a partition in his brain. On one side is friendship and affection; on the other is the urge to excel and win. Winning. That's the bottom line.

Y. A. also had a tennis partner in San Francisco he thought might help the team. Matt Hazeltine was thirty-six years old at the time and he had been out of the game for a full season. His credentials were laden with All-Pro honors, and his service as defensive captain of the 49ers had been long and honorable. But Matt had suffered some knee trouble and his advancing age had caused his replacement. He had quit the game for private business and was contented and in fine shape. But he was willing to give a comeback a try with the Giants. I can remember Matt appearing at training camp in as excellent physical condition as any man on the field. He was turned on about playing again and one day during the exhibition season he went to Jimmy Garrett, our special team coach, and said, "Jimmy, I don't want to not make this football team because you might think I'm not willing to play on the special teams. You put me on any team and I'll play. I'll run down on kickoffs, block for punts and field goals; you name it, because I want to play football." You can imagine the kind of effect this had on our younger players. Here is a great player like Matt Hazeltine so switched on by the game that he is willing to play with the so-called "suicide squads," so how could they look on such chores with disdain?

After one of the early exhibition games, I asked Matt how he felt to be back. He peeled off a muddy shirt and looked at me with a wide smile spread across his face, "It's great!" he said. "You know, some guys are born to be business tycoons or painters or something, but me, I was born to play football. I'll tell you, Fran, just between you and me, I'd rather play football than screw!"

Bob Tucker was hardly an All-Pro when he was signed by the Giants, but he loved the game enough to labor for a full season with a semi-pro team called the Pottstown (Pennsylvania) Firebirds. The Philadelphia Eagles had taken

a look at Tucker the year before and cut him. He had returned to Pottstown convinced that his shot at the pros was
past. The Giants gave him one more try and, as it turned
out, nearly missed him like the Eagles. Only after we'd tried
a number of veterans at tight end did we decide to give
Tucker a cursory look in a late exhibition game before re-
leasing him. He was great, showing extraordinary ability as a
blocker and short-pass receiver—which is all one can expect
from a tight end. But Tucker offered bonuses in being able to
go on deep patterns and to run with the ball once he'd caught
it. It makes me shudder every time I think how close we
came to cutting him and I can only ponder how many other
tremendous players have slipped out of the pros because they
had a bad day during that brief spell they had to prove themselves. We remember the ones who were salvaged—John
Unitas, "Big Daddy" Gene Lipscomb, "Fuzzy" Thurston, etc.
—but whom did we miss? We'll never know.

At any rate, we had Tucker and he, along with Ron
Johnson and Clifton McNeil, were to become three of our
four top pass receivers. The Giants' success at wheeling and
dealing had been unbelievable, as if the law of averages had
finally compensated for all those years of blundering and ill
fortune. It in essence made our team, having provided our
starting lineup with two first-rank linebackers and a pair of
quality defensive tackles, a star-quality tight end, a speedy,
battle-proven wide receiver and an All-Pro, 1000-yard rusher
and pass catcher. For that we had given up a few reserves
and some low-draft choices. Who could ask for more?

As training camp approached, we knew that time was
our greatest enemy. With the inevitable injuries that would
arise and other uncertainties that are certainties in pro ball,
Alex and his coaches figured that as many as six defensive
positions would be occupied by new faces (with only Spider

Lockhart, Willie Williams, Bob Lurtsema, Fred Dryer, and Scott Eaton apparently locked in), while as many as five new men appeared likely to penetrate the starting offense. What we needed—especially the defense—was the time to work together, to develop that fluid sensation of oneness that exists on all winning teams. We would have that time if the increasingly bellicose talk between the Players Association and the owners didn't materialize into a strike.

VI

_____

By the time July 15 rolled around, I was primed and ready for the 1970 season. I'd been running hard each day and playing a great deal of golf. I was in excellent physical shape despite having passed that so-called barrier of thirty. Some people might think that's a ticket to oblivion in professional sports, but for an NFL quarterback it symbolizes that maybe—just maybe—he's got enough experience under his belt so that he can start operating at his peak. Very few quarterbacks are as good on the short side of thirty as they are on the long side, and with me about to start my tenth season in the pros, I figured this might be a great year.

We were a hopeful football team, what with the tremendous trades and drafts that Alex, Wellington Mara and the coaching staff had pulled off, but we knew that the time remaining to integrate the new players and establish the new offensive system was at a premium. Right to the last minute I hoped our Players Association would make a settlement with the owners and permit us to report to camp on time. But that was not to be, and while I lazed through three unexpected weeks of playing golf when I expected to be in training camp, a vast majority of the Giants, including me, supported the walkout. It was a tough thing for us to do,

because nobody wanted the dispute, which centered on retirement benefits. But once our Players Association had made
the judgment of calling the delay in reporting to camp, we
were behind them to the bitter end. That is not to say the
walkout received uniformly strong backing across the league.
Some clubs, namely the Jets, the Oakland Raiders and the
Dallas Cowboys faltered in their resolve to buck the threats
of their owners. In fact, the Cowboys' management had set
a rather ominous precedent in strikebreaking. Its last four
player representatives to the association had been traded
and the job was so unpopular that each year the team had
trouble finding a candidate. Other guys on other teams were
afraid to support the strike too, lest they incur the wrath
of their owners and coaches. That was nonsense, because I
learned very early in my sports career that the only place
anybody gets judged is on the playing field, and all the apple-
polishing in the world isn't going to save your job if somebody can do it better.

I have to give them credit; the owners did an effective
job in getting their case across to the public and to the
players. Because a segment of the daily press is literally a
captive of the big-time sports management—little more than
press agents without a portfolio (after all, how many lunches,
trips and cases of booze do you think the players buy writers
each year?). It began to look as if our player representatives
belonged in the same prison with Jimmy Hoffa. Meanwhile
the owners were sales-pitching the less-established players,
telling them it was perfectly all right for a Gale Sayers or a
John Brodie or a John Unitas or a Dick Butkus to hold out
because they could come to camp at the last minute and be
guaranteed of a job. But, they claimed, the "little guys," the
reserve guards and tackles, etc., were really being hurt by

the strike because they had no guarantee of employment and needed all the time in camp they could get.

To counteract this, some of the better-known players and I called a press conference in New York. Gale Sayers, John Brodie and a few other stars showed up. So did a fair representation of the press, including Howard Cosell of ABC and Frank Gifford of CBS. NBC never appeared. Our argument was as follows: Sure, we're pretty well set to play, but more important, we've also got enough income and enough outside investments so that we don't have to worry when our careers are over. But what about the guy who labors in the pit Sunday after Sunday for half the pay and recognition? What about him when he leaves the game? He was the man the Players Association was fighting for. We thought we got our point across, although there was far from unanimity throughout the twenty-six teams. Even the Giants had a man who sided with the owners. He was our kicker, Pete Gogolak, the club's resident Right Winger. After the players' press conference, Wellington Mara gathered the team together to try to explain his position and to persuade them to return to camp. He was extremely fair, I must say, although Wellington again stressed the owners' contention that the so-called superstars were risking the careers of the lesser-known players while taking no chances themselves. After the meeting broke up, Peter made a pitch to a group of the guys about why they all should get back into harness.

Randy Minniear, one of the reserve running backs, asked Pete, "Gogy, just why are you so hot to get the strike over and get back to camp?"

Pete thought a minute and said, partly in jest, I think, "You're right, Randy. I'm like Gale Sayers, I don't have anything to worry about."

That did it. Because Pete was such a high-strung guy,

because of his politics and because he was maybe the most ungainly-looking athlete in football, he was always being ribbed anyway, but that crack really cost him dearly. For the rest of the training camp, Gogy was known as "Gale."

Finally the dispute was settled and we rushed off to the C. W. Post College campus for a three-day cram course before our exhibition season opened against the Packers in Green Bay. We had made our point, I think, and the entire experience, although unpleasant, had been worth it. I think it's to the credit of our coaches and our ownership that the strike was *never* mentioned after we reached camp. Not even a casual reference was made of the affair; never a snide remark or even an oblique pun. It was business as usual and that made our chore of gathering up the pieces a good bit easier. Unlike a lot of established teams whose lineups were relatively stable, we had perhaps eleven uncertain positions out of the twenty-two offensive and defensive starters to decide *plus* the injection of the new passing attack that end coach Joe Walton and Y. A. Tittle had been laboring over for much of the winter.

In the old days of pro football, a quarterback like Sammy Baugh might say to his favorite end, Bones Taylor, "Now, Bones, I want you to go down 12 yards, do a square-out, and I'll hit you." That was the pass play. With a good arm like Baugh's throwing to a good pair of hands like Taylor's against the primitive man-to-man coverage of the time, the odds were favorable they could come up with a completion. But as the defenses evolved into sophisticated zones, the passing attack was forced to develop into carefully diagramed routes for the receivers. You can recall the television color men talking at length about "primary" and "secondary" receivers and how a good quarterback might throw to a secondary man if his primary man was covered, or how he might call an "audible" play change at the line of scrimmage if the coverage wasn't to his liking or if he saw a blitz (or "red dog," as it used to be called) materializing.

That, unfortunately, is all bunk in today's football environment. There are no more primary and secondary receivers. The audible at the line of scrimmage is almost a thing of the past; I call no more than two or three a game. The reason is simple. Today's defenses are so subtle that a quarterback cannot call a play based on what he *thinks* they are going to do. He cannot gamble. Coming to the line of scrimmage, I can't tell whether the defense is going to play a zone defense that rolls to the strong side, or one that rolls to the weak side. They may play man-to-man, or they may play one-half man-to-man and one-half zone. Therefore the play I call must be capable of handling all contingencies. On a pass play, every back or end who goes down the field is a "primary" receiver. I wait for the defense *to tell me,* on the basis of their movements, which one of my men is going to get the ball. This is called a "key system" and for the most part uses the middle linebacker as the man who will dictate my target. In other words, I have a number of receivers all of whom are running exactly predetermined pass routes. In the few seconds after the ball is snapped, it is up to me to determine—solely on the basis of the movement of the defense in general and the middle linebacker in particular—which one of my men will be open or at least will have man-to-man coverage. If I can get the ball to him, chances are we will have a completion.

Walton's and Tittle's intent was to create for us a disciplined short-passing game, which in turn is crucial to developing the ball-control offense. Until they went to work, we had limited capability for passing to the off-side pattern. In other words, if we called a pass play to the weak side, chances are our strong-side receivers had nothing to do and were not prepared to take the pass if our "primary" receivers were covered. The new system was through a simple set of numerical combinations and gave each back and end an exact route to run on *every* pass play and therefore gave me tremendous options. Each passing play was designed to handle the blitz and because I knew I had between three and five potential receivers *every* time, I could get the ball away quicker, which meant I could get away with less pass-blocking protection.

There wasn't anything revolutionary in what Joe and Y. A. created; it simply increased the discipline, coordination and flexibility of our offense. So much has been said about the complexity of the game of football that some people must believe it takes a doctor of physics just to figure out your locker combination. Only geniuses need apply, is the popular superstition. That's hokum. The only geniuses in football are the men who perfect simplicity. It remains a game of simple execution—throwing, catching, kicking and most important, blocking and tackling. Do these things with a minimum of mistakes and you will have a winning football team even if it's populated with guys so stupid they read stop signs for entertainment. The more complex the offense or defense, the more chances for making mistakes, especially in times of high stress. Our plays have to be designed to take into account not only the smartest but the dumbest players on the team. The plays must be simple.

It is part of football lore that a quarterback has maybe three hundred plays crammed into his brain and he and his ten cohorts can execute each one to perfection at any given moment. That's very flattering, but nonsense. The New York Giants, like most pro teams, enter a game with possibly six or eight basic pass plays and twelve to fourteen running plays ready for use. However, as I will explain, we can use almost

infinite disguises on those plays based on the offensive formations we present. To begin with, we give our offensive men
numerical designations. The quarterback is "1," the halfback
"2," the fullback "3" (when lined up in the "brown" formation behind center, and "4" when he's in the "red" formation
behind the strong side tackle). The tight end is numbered
"7," the split end "8" and the flanker back "9." Another set
of numbers relate to "holes," or spaces, in the line between
the center, guards and tackles. The "1-hole" is between the
center and the right tackle; the "2-hole" is between the center and the left tackle. The "3-hole" is between the right guard
and the right tackle; the "5-hole" between the right tackle
and the tight end; the "7-hole" lies between the tight end and
the flanker, and the "9-hole" is out at the very end—desig-
nating an end-around. While the odd-numbered holes are
on the strong side, the even-numbered holes are on the
weak side and operate in the same sequence. Our running
plays include a power series, a trap series, dives, folds, slants
and sweeps and each has a specific blocking assignment for
everybody. For example, I can call, "Sweep 25," which tells
our team the following: The 2-back, or halfback, is going to
run to the 5-hole (hence "25"). The linemen, etc., know
exactly what their blocking assignments are on *all* sweep
series, so they are ready. If Ron Johnson or Joe Morrison is at
halfback, he knows he's going to run a sweep action play.
Now I can vary the formation, *i.e.,* "red right, double wing,
sweep 25, trap," which merely places our fullback in the
"red" position, Johnson in the double-wing slot (off the left
hip of the left guard), and tells the guards to trap-block, but
the basic play is *exactly the same.* I can call, "Brown right,
fullback peel, sweep 25, trap," which places the fullback behind me, sends him in motion to the weak side (peel), and
we will still run *precisely the same play,* with the halfback

sweeping to the right side, penetrating the line between the right tackle and the tight end. In other words, any number of running plays involving either the halfback or the fullback can be run through any number of holes in the line, from any number of offensive formations, with such filips as men in motion, pitchouts, fakes, etc., by simply calling a two-digit series of numbers.

The same is true of pass plays. Let's look at an "84 pass." All "80 series" pass plays relate to the flankerback (they don't necessarily make him any more important as a potential pass receiver, but they offer a simple point of reference for telling the rest of the team what to do). Another set of numbers, 1–10, describe specific pass patterns; "1" is a short square-in; "2" is a turn-in, etc. Say I call an "83 pass"; this immediately tells the flanker to go downfield 10 yards and square-in; the tight end and flanker go down 14 yards and curl in toward the middle while the two running backs run short "shoot" patterns out of the backfield, angling around the offensive guards. Each man does exactly the same thing on all "83 pass" calls, regardless of whether we send men in motion, use the I-formation, the stacked-I (where the flanker lines up, third in line, behind the halfback and the fullback), the double wing or whatever. *That never changes,* nor does it on "73 pass," "92 pass" or what have you. Each call gives each man a specific pattern to run and when he hears those two numbers in the huddle, he knows exactly what to do. And I know exactly where he's going. We play football by rules and if those rules never change, no matter how many tricky little formations we use to confuse the defense, the play should work.

We switched from the cadence signal call at the line of scrimmage to a noncadence call. In other words, instead of calling, "hut—hut—hut" in regular, measured beats, we switched to a random "hut, hut—hut——hut" call, which is designed to keep the defense off balance. In the heat of a game, a quarterback—all quarterbacks—tend to pick a certain number and persist in using it to start the play. For instance, if I kept starting my plays with "Hut 1, hut 2," it wouldn't take long before all the defensive linemen and linebackers would get my rhythm and start blowing in on me at practically the same count. To prevent this, and to offer me a bit more time to look over the defense, we went to the non-cadence call. It worked most of the time—on a few occasions brilliantly—and it failed on one particularly disastrous occasion that I can recall.

Let's run through a typical huddle-and-play execution. I have called, "Dive 23, motion, on 3. Break!" This is a simple off-guard running play by the halfback with the fullback in motion. The play will be called on count of three. When I say "Break," the team has headed for its offensive set at the line of scrimmage. As I walk toward the center, I am examining the defense, trying to spot any significant changes in their setup that I can exploit. Once in position, I shout, "Set!," which places all the players in their stances, ready for the snap. I then shout a *one-digit number, followed by a two-digit number*. This means nothing *unless* I repeat the snap count, which means the two-digit number that follows will be a new play—an audible, if you will. Therefore, if everything looks good and I decide to follow through with the play I called in the huddle, I will call, "Four" (which means nothing), "62!" (which is also meaningless) "—hut 1— hut 2!," at which point the ball is snapped and the play is underway. Now, if I come to the line of scrimmage and see an obvious weakness, for example, which I want to exploit with a pass, I might shout "Set, 3" (everybody's ears perk up then, because I've repeated the snap count I called in the huddle) "72!" That's the new play! simply because my repetition of the "three" snap-count has cancelled the original "Dive 23, motion" I called in the huddle. I then continue on with my count, "Hut 1—hut 2;" when the ball is centered and our new pass play unfolds.

Sound complicated? It's not, really. Once a player has worked with the system a few days it all becomes very simple. But he's got to pay attention—that's essential.

As I said, the nonrhythmic call can work great, like it was to work for us in the second St. Louis game in 1970. We expected their great free safety, Larry Wilson, to try a bunch of safety blitzes that afternoon and here's the way the new count helped. On one play I began my count and saw Larry edging toward the line of scrimmage. "He's coming with the blitz!" I thought to myself. I was into the count, "Hut 1—— hut 2. . . ." I made a great, long pause, maybe six seconds. Larry, his chance to blitz—which depends on his hitting the line almost at the same time the ball is snapped—blunted, hesitantly began to move back. For that instant that he was off balance I completed my call, "Hut 3, hut 4," and managed to catch him a few strides out of position. The pass play went for a touchdown.

Then sometimes it doesn't work. Take the same game, early in the second quarter with us in near midfield and needing a first down. We needed three yards and I thought I'd be cute. In the huddle I laid down my plan, "Now listen you guys, we need only three yards, so I'm going to try to draw them offsides with a trick count. Now here's how I'm going to call it: "Hut—hut——hut—*hut!*" You got that? O.K., Dive 34 on 4! And remember the count! We went to the line, set up, and I began my call, "Hut—hut . . . !"

Boom! Doug Van Horn, our right guard, powered offside, knocking a Cardinal sprawling. Whistles blew, yellow flags flew everywhere. Doug Van Horn, a cool, five-year veteran—

a man who *never* jumps offside, just jumped offside. In his eagerness to work with the tricky cadence, he just plain blew it, as we all can blow it sometimes when we try too hard. Rather than third and three, it became third and eight, and as I slogged back to the huddle I could recall five other times that I tried the same play. Each time, one of *my own* players had jumped the gun. Like the man said, keep it simple.

That we had to do for the opening exhibition game with Green Bay. With three days to work, we were lucky to develop half a dozen pass plays and eight to ten running plays before leaving for Wisconsin. We weren't terribly optimistic about a polished performance, which didn't bother me a great deal. I feel the entire fuss about exhibition, or "pre-season" games, as they are now called, is absurd. The first one of the encounters I played in was in 1961, when the Vikings met the Dallas Cowboys in Sioux Falls, South Dakota. We played in a ten-thousand-seat stadium. Five thousand people showed up, indicating we weren't the biggest thing even in Sioux Falls! Times have changed. "Pre-season" games are part of the season-ticket package with most teams, and a majority of them are sellouts. The press and television give them much the same coverage as regular games, and they along with the public show up expecting to see the big studs—the starting teams—play against each other. There isn't any chance for football teams to conceal themselves in a corner of Florida the way the baseball guys do. Everything is out front and people make a very big deal about it, including the players. Don't forget, Allie Sherman lost his job, as have other coaches, on the basis of bad exhibition seasons. However, they still don't mean a thing in the end. In 1970 the Dallas Cowboys had a disastrous pre-season schedule, losing about everything except their fancy silver pants. They got to the Super Bowl.

In 1964 the Cleveland Browns won the NFL Championship after failing to win a single exhibition game!

Vince Lombardi said you should win everything you play. He said that during the glory years of the Packers, when he had enough horsepower *to win* everything he played. He said that with the Redskins too, but it didn't make any difference; they still lost. The exhibition season was, and still is, the only time a team gets to experiment with new plays and personnel in actual game conditions and I think it should be viewed in that context only.

Two days before we departed for Green Bay, Freddie Dryer rolled into camp. He'd driven his VW bus from California and the trip had taken longer than expected. He was in great shape and ready to play, but he was late and Alex levied a two-hundred-dollar fine on him for the tardiness. Then there was his hair. The pro coaches had come a long way from requiring that the guys wear brush cuts and warm-up jackets, but Fred was operating at the outer limit of their tolerance. His thick, sun-bleached blond locks reached to his shoulders and that was more than they could handle. Y. A. Tittle was delegated to approach Freddie with a deal; if he would get his hair cut—crew-cut length was the stipulation—the two-hundred-dollar fine would be forgotten. Fred balked but did appear at the barber shop in the Northland Hotel in Green Bay to get at least some of the foliage shorn. Not enough, said the coaches. The fine stood.

Green Bay played their horses, Nitschke, Robinson, Bart Starr, Donny Anderson, Fred Carr, *et al.*, for most of the game. I played the first half, operating for the most part with our front line personnel, and we ended the second quarter owning a 14–7 lead. We experimented for the rest of the game, letting rookie Eddie Baker operate at quarterback. Green Bay kept up the pressure and blitzed the youngster like crazy. Eddie, who was destined for our taxi squad in 1970, did a good job, but rookies just can't handle a guy like Ray Nitschke. Our second and third stringers slowly gave way in the face of the Green Bay thrust and we lost in the fourth quarter. But we were pleased. We'd moved the ball well, and our starters seemed to have been more than a match for theirs in the first half. We were especially pleased with Jim Files's performance at linebacker; he was playing his first game for us and seemed to support the hopes and expectations we'd placed in him.

The Jets came next and we owed them one. The score was 28–24, although we led at one point 28–0. Unfortunately, Namath didn't play, so the victory wasn't quite as satisfying as it might have been.

Dick Shiner, whom we planned to use as backup quarterback, played the entire game against his old team, Pittsburgh. We lost, but again a lot of our new guys were getting christened to the NFL and we were far from discouraged. Shiner (or "Slugger," as we call him) has one of the most powerful arms in football (he can throw a ball 60 yards standing flat-footed) and a tremendous knowledge of the game. He was a great deal of help to me in developing tactics within the new offense and made me confident that we had a competent man to lead the team if I was injured. Dick seems to have all the equipment to be a great quarterback—good size, fine arms, proper attitude, etc., but he's never been able to make it as regular starter. But as far as I was concerned, his affability, his technical awareness of the game and his great ability as a holder for Pete Gogolak made him a decided asset to our team.

We lost again to San Diego, once more building up an early lead and turning things over to our newer players. They squeezed by us, 30–27, but we didn't consider the outcome

Need anyone say more about the Rams game? Fearsome Onesome Merlin Olsen bears down while Doug Van Horn (63) and Tucker Frederickson (24) wait for me to join them on the Yankee Stadium grass.

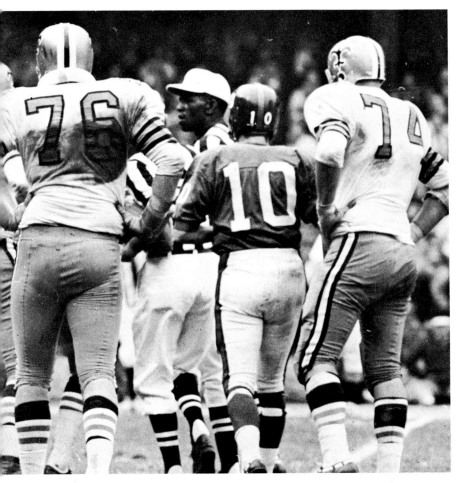

Fools rush in where angels fear to tread. I protest a decision in the 1969 Saints game despite the presence of Dave Rowe (76) and Mike Tilleman (74), each of whom is six inches taller than I and outweighs me by *ninety* pounds.

With Allie Sherman at the press conference announcing my trade to the Giants.

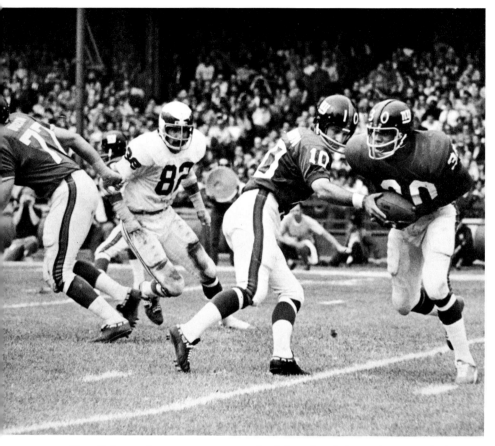

Ron Johnson begins a sweep to the left side while Rich Buzin (77) heads downfield. The Eagles' Tim Rossovich (82) is zeroing in on Ronnie.

Jerry Shay (75), Jim Files (58) and Spider Lockhart (43) marshal their strength for another onslaught from the Rams' offense during the final game of 1970.

Bob Tucker formally announces his arrival in New York. The sensational rookie tight end scores the first of two touchdowns against the Cardinals in Yankee Stadium.

Matt Hazeltine (64) loses his helmet in the process of nailing the Jets' George Nock after a short gain. Jim Files (58) adds the finishing touches while Tommy Longo (44) moves in to assist.

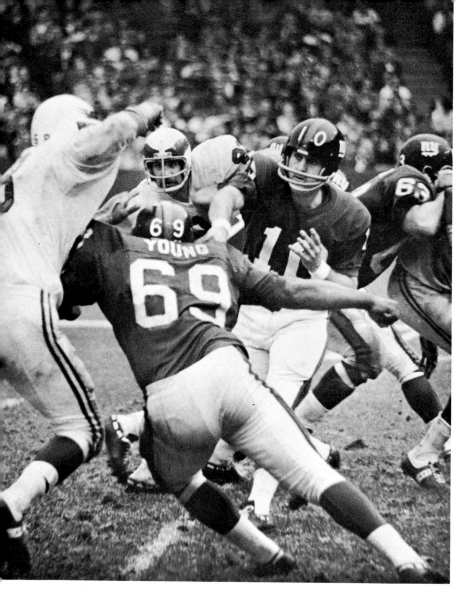

Willie Young blocks the Eagles' Mel Tom during a pass play in the first 1970 Philadelphia game.

Alex Webster and I discuss strategy in the heat of the 1969 season. Joe Walton and Gary Wood (9) also take part in the discussion.

Staying loose prior to the Rams game. Alex Webster (left foreground) presides over a relaxed team meeting in the Yankee Stadium locker room. Front row, left to right: Joe Morrison (barefoot), Greg Larson, Doug Van Horn, Charlie Harper, myself, Willie Williams. Second row, left to right: Willie Young, Pete Case, Rich Buzin, Dennis Craig, Eddie Baker, Bob Lurtsema. Background, left to right: Otto Brown (in striped shirt), Bob Tucker (seated), Tucker Frederickson (standing), Ron Johnson (seated), Dick Shiner, Ernie Koy, Don Herrmann, Jerry Shay.

Rich Buzin does his best to hold off the Eagles' Tim Rossovich. Funny, but it looks as if Rich has a grip on Tim's shirt. But how can that be? After all, holding is illegal.

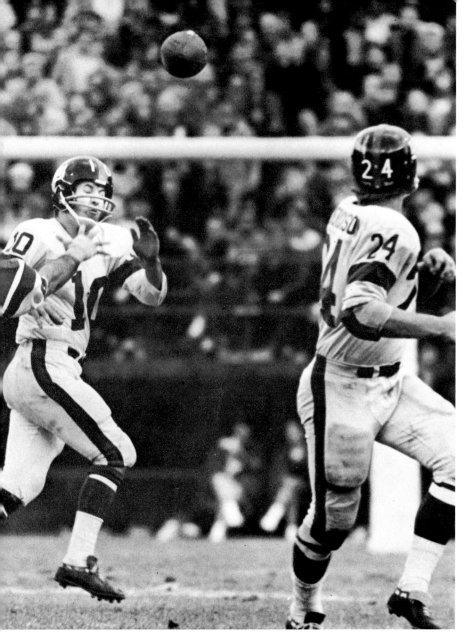

John Elliott of the Jets is just a shade too late in trying to bat away a short toss to Tucker Frederickson.

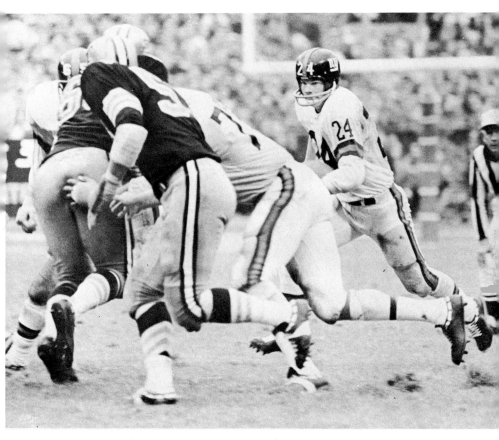

Pete Case leads a sweep to the right side for Tucker Frederickson during the 1970 New Orleans game.

The regular Johnson-Tucker post-practice chess epic is carried on despite my nearby conversation with a pair of reporters.

Should I call it scrambling? In any case, I'm trying to outrun the Cowboys' Chuck Howley in the second 1970 game with the Cowboys.

Ron Johnson breaks free of the Philadelphia secondary for a 60-yard touchdown run on our second offensive play from scrimmage. The score led us to our first victory of the 1970 season.

All photographs courtesy of the New York Football Giants

important, mainly because both the offense and defense seemed to be materializing as workable entities and we felt stronger than we had in years. One of the reasons was a spare, thoughtful man from New Jersey named Jimmy Garrett. Jimmy had come to us from the staff of the Cowboys to head our special teams—the punting, field-goal, point-after-touchdown and kickoff units that can be so important to victory. Although most people—including a majority of coaches—tend to ignore this aspect of the game and throw in a hodgepodge of bench warmers for such thankless duty, up to 20 *per cent* of all the plays a team executes in a given game may involve the special units. For years the Giants had ranked near the bottom in all special-team categories. Nobody could remember when a Giant had run back a punt for a touchdown, for example. Garrett, whose knowledge of football was encyclopedic, set out to change all this. While most teams devote no more than an hour a week to this aspect of the game, Jimmy worked us twenty minutes a day, in addition to operating a long blackboard session each Tuesday. They were so well organized, so articulate and so interesting that they had become a highlight of practice. One day Matt Hazeltine cracked, "Jimmy, your talks are so good they remind me of President Roosevelt's Fireside Chats."

Somebody yelled across the room, "Matt, you're the only guy old enough to *remember* President Roosevelt's Fireside Chats!"

It had begun to work by the middle of the exhibition season, thanks to Garrett and his number-one special-team operative, "Mean Joe Green from Bowling Green." Joe was our key man for every kickoff, field goal, etc. Ostensibly Spider Lockhart's backup, "Mean Joe," at 5' 11", 185 pounds, was pound for pound the strongest man I've ever encountered. A wrestling champion and phenomenal middle linebacker at

Bowling Green, Joe had the kind of "Katie, bar the door" attitude that was perfect for the blitzkreig tactics of special-team situations. He was a great boost for our spirits and his aggressiveness led Garrett to comment, "It's a good thing Joe can play football; otherwise he'd be in a helluva fight every night of his life."

As training camp and pre-season play gained intensity, injuries and the appearance of new prospects began to change and solidify what was to be our starting lineup. Defensively, Wesley Grant was hurt in practice and it was doubtful he could return for the remainder of the year. Bob Lurtsema was moved from defensive tackle to defensive end. The other expected starter at defensive tackle, Jim Kanicki, was benched with injuries most of training camp, although he was still being counted for the opener against the Chicago Bears. John Kirby, a seven-year veteran, had spent much of the season operating as outside linebacker, but with the passage of each day it became more obvious that he would lose his starting assignment to Matt Hazeltine. Our strong safety, Tom Longo, had taken over when our sixty-nine regular, old Detroit Lion Bruce Maher, had a dispute with the coaching staff and was not rehired. Tommy, with very little experience at the position, played a great game against the Jets, then broke his wrist and left us in an uncertain position for the regular season.

There were some changes on offense as well. Bob Tucker, as I mentioned, came out of nowhere to take the tight end job away from Aaron Thomas, Butch Wilson, Rick Kotite, and Freeman White. Until the Philadelphia exhibition game, which we won easily, I'd barely paid any attention to him. I'll bet I hadn't thrown him more than half-dozen balls during the entire camp. Then he appeared in the field and blocked like an All-Pro. The job was his, although his physical appearance

—rather loose-jointed, gangly and smallish-looking for a tight end—very nearly forced us to overlook him. It's that "super-man" distraction we have in football where we all become deluded by the sheer physical presence of some players, when less-imposing guys like Bob Tucker come into their own only when the whistle blows. Finally there is the case of Joe Morrison—a situation that caused all of us a great deal of concern. Here was Joe, the man with eleven years of guts and effort for the Giants, a great football player in every sense, our offensive captain, coming off his best season and about to be beaten out of his starting position by Ron Johnson. Johnson was brilliant—a perfect man for our new offense with the quickness, intelligence and instincts to become one of the best runners in the game. But what about Joe? Some people call football heartless and dehumanized, but I wish they could have witnessed the consternation and worry that Alex and the coaches went through, trying to find a berth for Joe. They felt they owed it to him. He was tried at flanker and split end; even at fullback. But Joe was a halfback. So was Ron Johnson, a man eleven years Joe's junior and immeasurably faster. Somehow, we had to face the reality that Joe Morrison was going to ride the bench in 1970.

Our last exhibition game was against Cleveland at Yankee Stadium and with our starting lineups about solidified, we played all-out football for the entire sixty minutes. The Browns were long-time rivals and we wanted to go into our first regular season game against the Bears on an up note. Therefore we played for real, as did Cleveland. With less than a minute left we scored to go ahead by two points and it looked as though we had a win in our pockets. It was decided that our kickoff to the Browns, which was going to be made by Jim Norton, would be a "squib kick." Norton would hit the ball off the side of his foot, which would send it slicing a short distance downfield before it bounced crazily to the ground. The intent of such a kick was to keep it out of the hands of the opposition's kickoff return specialists and prevent them from setting up a runback play that might spring a man loose for a touchdown. The "squib kick" didn't "squib." It caromed off Norton's shoe and flopped lazily a few yards before a Brown fell on it near midfield. With a few seconds left on the clock the Browns passed themselves within field-goal range, where Don Cockroft kicked a three-pointer to win.

We were sore. We'd blown the game with the damn "squib kick," and the locker room was full of griping and self-recrimination. In retrospect, we made far too much out of the entire incident, but it did end our exhibition season on a sour note and served to send us into the opener against the Bears with a bad taste in our mouths. The mental aspects of football remain a mystery to me, but I am inclined to believe that if that Browns game had ended the way we had intended it to, our 1970 season might have been even more successful than it was.

VII

WITH THE 1970 New York Giant season about to open with a night game against the Chicago Bears, the final cuts to a forty-man squad had been made. A few guys were placed on waivers, others were shunted off to the taxi squad and a couple were put on the disabled list. Forty football players remained, maybe not the strongest squad in the NFL but certainly the toughest, tightest, best-spirited collection of men the Giants had fielded in many years. From that group would rise heroes and goats, game breakers and goof-offs, All-Pros and clowns, each of whom would in one way or another have his say in the Giants' destiny.

For better or worse, these were the thirty-odd frontline players and coaches who would carry the Giants wherever they were going to go.

COACHING STAFF

HEAD COACH: Alex Webster, former Giant fullback, beginning his first full season as the team's leader—and a highly unconventional one at that. Alex was a pure, outfront individual, full of emotion and naturalness. He had come from his brawling youth in Northern New Jersey to greatness with the Giants without acquiring much nuance or subtlety. Alex said what he felt had to be said, did what he felt had to be done. I can recall a time when he was giving a speech at a banquet in Connecticut and a front-row heckler began to get on his nerves. Finally Alex couldn't stand it anymore. His face a glaze of crimson and his great neck muscles bulging, he strode off the stage and barged to the table of his tormentor. "Listen, mister, these people paid me to come up here and talk to them and not listen to your crap. Either you shut up and quit abusing me or we'll step outside and settle this!" That was pure Alex in action and it was his sincerity and directness that endeared him to the team and gave us a sense of unity. For better or for worse, Alex Webster was one of us.

OFFENSIVE COACH: Ken Kavanaugh, with seventeen years on the Giants' staff, had seen it all. He had a coolness that came only with maturity and a complete understanding of one's surroundings—in Ken's case, professional football. A college All-American at LSU, Ken had played end on the great Chicago Bear teams of the 1940s before coming to the Giants' staff. The man who ran the blackboard session each Tuesday and worked as the press box spotter during games, Ken managed to maintain an even keel in the most trying situations. While most players and younger coaches refuse to accept the prospect of defeat under any circumstances, cool, intelligent men like Ken have had the raw edges of simple, combative optimism eroded away and have come to accept the inevitability of losing as well as winning. Not that Ken was a defeatist; nothing could be farther from the truth. It was simply that he, more than the rest of us, was able to take the bad bounces, the miscues and the dumb mistakes in stride and keep working toward that better day that experience had taught him would surely come.

OFFENSIVE LINE COACH: Roosevelt Brown, a stalwart of the great Giant teams and one of the premier offensive linemen in the history of professional football. A twentieth-round draft choice from little Morgan State, Rosie came to All-Pro status as a punishing 6′ 3″, 255-pound tackle. His athletic ability was so complete that the Giants' coaches used him extensively on goal line stands—a deceivingly difficult job for an offensive specialist. Rosie came to the coaching staff after phlebitis cut short his playing career, and immediately became a fixture on the staff. Because Rosie had a knack for butchering the pronunciation of any name, he naturally called the roll for each morning's practice. Joe Szczecko (pronounced "Shesh-ko") was inevitably Joe "Check-o," etc., etc., which made Rosie's muster a high point of every day.

OFFENSIVE END COACH: Joe Walton, whose intense, feisty play at tight end for the Giants during the glory days had carried over into his coaching. His fierce combativeness caused him to be caustic in his criticism of players (if Joe Walton described you as a "banana," you knew you were in for trouble). He was a fine strategist and was largely responsible for the new play terminology being used for the first time. He, more than any single person, deserved credit for our greatly improved passing game.

DEFENSIVE COACH: Norb Hecker had come to the Giants via an assistant's position with Lombardi at Green Bay and the head coaching job with the Atlanta Falcons (where he'd been succeeded by Van Brocklin). A conservative, methodical man who preferred the kind of bulldog execution taught by Lombardi, Norb had adjusted to the demands of the Giant situation where he simply didn't have the manpower to overwhelm the opposition. He effectively switched his thinking to include more blitzing and defensive deception in order to better utilize the talent he had. Norb was an intelligent and capable professional whose involvement with the game ranged back to his playing days as a defensive back and place kicker.

DEFENSIVE LINE COACH: Jim Katcavage—the "Kat," as he was known—played defensive end in New York along with Hall of Famer Andy Robusstelli during the championship era. The prototype brush-cut, hard-hat, Marine-tough-guy football player, Kat brought a childlike love of football to his job. He had great spirit, and the traditions, hopes and aspirations of the Giant football team seemed to be the most important things in his life.

DEFENSIVE BACKFIELD COACH: Emlen Tunnell, very probably the greatest safety ever, holds numerous all-time records, including 79 interceptions and 2,209 yards on punt returns. His fame was established with the Giants from 1948 to 1958, although he ended his career with a Green Bay championship team in 1961. A relaxed, easygoing guy whose byword was "different strokes for different folks," Emlen was the first black to play on the Giants and one of the first to enter the NFL. A devoted poster maker, Emlen and scout Jim Trimble were forever hanging drawings, press clippings, slogans and admonishments around the locker room. It was not unusual to arrive on the field at Yankee Stadium for practice before a big game and find several full-size drawings of the opposition's stars glowering down at us from some upper-deck seats, thanks to Emlen. A fixture on the team, it was said that a grateful Mara family had guaranteed Emlen a job in the Giant organization for as long as he desired.

SPECIAL-TEAMS COACH: Jimmy Garrett, a great thinker and strategist of football as well as a pure fan. Garrett's impact on the team is discussed earlier.

THE OFFENSE

CENTER: Greg Larson, age thirty-one, 6′ 3″, 250 pounds. Known as "Igor" among the team, the nickname was applied by Tucker Frederickson because of Greg's strongly Swedish background. Beginning his tenth year, Larson came to the Giants in 1961 and played offensive tackle briefly before Ray Wietecha's retirement. His recovery from a 1965 knee injury (suffered in a punting play on a block by Rip Hawkins, who at the time was my roommate) was one of the most courageous stories in football. A prideful leader in the line, he had not missed a game since 1967. I personally had great confidence in his ability to advise me about the course of the running attack. Very large and strong for a center, Greg was not quite as quick as he had been before his knee injury, but he remained All-Pro caliber.

RIGHT GUARD: Doug Van Horn, age twenty-seven, 6′ 2″, 245 pounds. "Reggie," as we called him (for no good reason), had exhibited tremendous fortitude during his short, frustrating pro career. An All-American at Ohio State, he was drafted second by the Detroit Lions in 1966 and arrived late in camp owing to the All-Star game. After riding the bench for much of the year, he was tardy for camp again in 1967, because of National Guard duty, and the Lions cut him.

Picked up late by the Giants, he was assigned to the West-chester Bulls. Such a comedown for a former All-American might have been more than some men could have taken, but Doug pitched in and played like a demon for the taxi squad. Then, after being brought back to the Giants in 1968, he developed a heart murmur, which we feared might end his career. But treatment at the Mayo Clinic permitted him to return late in the season and he's been a stalwart for us ever since. Very quick and strong, with excellent balance that gave him exceptional ability to pull and run, Doug rated as our finest offensive lineman in 1969 and would very likely get All-Pro recognition if and when the Giants would win a championship.

LEFT GUARD: Pete Case, age twenty-nine, 6' 3", 245 pounds. "Ol' Goober" had been my roommate on road trips for a number of years, which makes sense since we were a couple of old Georgia Bulldogs. One year behind me in college, Pete and I played together on Georgia's Southeast Conference Championship team in 1959. Pete came up with the Eagles and started for them as a rookie in 1962. He was traded to the Giants in 1966 and had been a prized lineman ever since. Soft-spoken and emotional off the field, Pete ranked among the finest in the league as a zone blocker and pass protector.

RIGHT TACKLE: Rich Buzin, age twenty-five, 6' 4", 250 pounds. Rich was the callow youth of the offensive line as we started the season, having been drafted second behind Fred Dryer in 1969. A finely trained player from Joe Paterno's Penn State organization, Rich was still learning the nuances of the pro game. Dedicated and high-strung, he tended to be bothered by adversity, but that was expected to pass as he gained maturity, and he was in fact to turn into a helluva offensive tackle.

LEFT TACKLE: Willie Young, age twenty-seven, 5′ 10½″, 270 pounds. The "Sugar Bear" was one of my favorite people, thanks to his easy-going disposition and quiet sense of humor. Picked up as a free agent from Grambling by the Giants, Willie began his fifth years with the growing reputation as a punishing pass protector and blocker. The year before, he'd put the Bears' Lloyd Phillips out with a clean block—a rather rare feat for an interior offensive lineman. Despite his great girth, Willie possessed a set of the nimblest feet on the team.

Often in short-yardage situations I'd ask my lineman who could handle his man to get us the necessary yardage. Rich Buzin, enthusiastic and competitive as he was, would always announce that he could handle the job. Sometimes Rich could, sometimes he couldn't, but when I heard ol' "Sugar Bear" say, "I got it," I knew the yardage was there and I'd call the play through Willie's hole every time.

TIGHT END: Bob Tucker, age twenty-six, 6′ 2″, 220 pounds. I've mentioned Bob Tucker, the sleeper from the Pottstown Firebirds, before, but it should be repeated that he was to develop into one of the finest tight ends in the game thanks to his deadly blocking and consistent pass receiving. While it was planned to start the aging Aaron Thomas at tight end, in a simple deference to this fine player's long and devoted service to the Giants, there was little question that as the season progressed, Tucker would be a rising star in the offense.

SPLIT END: Clifton McNeil, age twenty-nine, 6' 2",
187 pounds. After a fine career as a quarterback at Grambling,
Clifton was drafted by the Cleveland Browns, converted to a
wide receiver and relegated to the bench as a backup for the
magnificent Paul Warfield. He was then traded in to the
49ers, where he led the NFL in receptions in 1968. Then
Clifton held out on his contract, was late in reporting to camp
in 1969 and got the San Francisco management on his back.
A very bright guy, Clifton was traded to us as one of the few
sub-ten-second sprinters in football who could cut effectively
(most can only run straight ahead at such speeds). He executed pass cuts as well as anybody in the game and he *liked*
to have the ball thrown to him. A fine public speaker, Clifton
was later in the season to take over Spider Lockhart's traditional job of giving the team prayer. One day, without warning, Clifton got up before a game and uttered a really excellent prayer. Spider had been using the same prayer for as
long as anybody could remember, but when we won that
day, Clifton got the job. He's so good at it I've threatened on
several occasions to get ol' Clifton a big tent and make ourselves a fortune on the southern revival circuit.

FLANKER BACK: Don Herrmann, age twenty-three,
6' 2", 195 pounds. We faced the Chicago game with a question
mark at flanker back. Some of the coaches preferred Rich
Houston (who would therefore start), and I favored Don
Herrmann. Rich was decisively faster (4.6 seconds vs. 4.9 seconds in the 40-yard dash), but I felt he had the natural skills
to be a great cornerback. On the other hand, Don, although
hardly a sprinter, had exceptional skill at cutting, jumping
and catching the ball. Rich had the edge as an open-field
runner, but I believed that like All-Pros Gary Collins or Jimmy
Orr, neither of whom are extraordinary runners, Don Herr-

mann could develop into one of the better flankers in football. This argument was to go unresolved for several weeks before Don won the job.

HALFBACK: Ron Johnson, age twenty-two, 6′ 1″, 205 pounds. As in the case of Aaron Thomas at tight end, Joe Morrison would be given the honor of starting at this position against the Bears, but the quickness, the intelligence, plus the exceptional running and pass catching ability of Ron Johnson made him a key figure in our plans. I have never played with a guy who learned faster than Ron. Although he was still learning to run pass patterns out of the backfield, something he had not done at Cleveland, he was obviously an instinctive runner; my first handoff to him in training camp had made that abundantly clear. A quiet but very personable guy, his post-practice chess games with Bob Tucker had become a clubhouse tradition even before the season started.

FULLBACK: Tucker Frederickson, age twenty-seven, 6′ 2″, 220 pounds. In case anybody thinks being a football star is easy, he should ponder the story of Tucker Frederickson. An All-American running back at Auburn, Tucker was the number-one draft choice in all football in 1965 and went to the Giants, thanks to their dismal showing the year previous. He had a great rookie year, both on and off the field, where he became a favorite with the fans in New York. Early in the 1966 training camp, Tucker was engaged in a "West Point" drill, in which an offensive lineman blocks one-and-one on a defensive lineman while running interference for a back. Tucker strained a knee ligament but continued to work out. Then, in the first exhibition game against the Packers, he tried to salvage a flare pass that had been thrown behind him and was gang-tackled while off balance. His knee was destroyed; both ligaments and cartilage were critically damaged. He was out for the entire season. After operations and a long, difficult rehabilitation program, he tried a comeback in 1967. When I met Tucker that year, this wonderfully likable guy was on the edge of despondency, unsure whether his career would continue. It did, for a few months. During a game with New Orleans he hurt his other knee, although not as seriously, and was out for the remainder of the year. He managed to play the full year in 1968 but not with the power and abandon he had enjoyed in 1965. He was sidelined for part of 1969 with a badly swollen ankle, but his freight-train running and superlative blocking in the 1970 exhibition season convinced everybody that Tucker had returned to full strength. What's more, Tucker's self-image of not being a pass receiver was to change radically. One of the best-liked players on the team, Tucker seemed ready to resume his standing as one of the finest fullbacks in the game.

QUARTERBACK: Myself, suddenly rather patriarchal at age thirty and feeling, at 193 pounds, as good as at any time in my career. I was backed up by Dick "Slugger" Shiner, as smart and strong a reserve quarterback as there was in the league.

THE DEFENSE

DEFENSIVE TACKLE: Jerry Shay, age twenty-seven, 6′ 2″, 245 pounds. Not large or particularly fast for a defensive tackle, Jerry brought tremendous persistence to his job. A furious, relentless kind of player who had been the Vikings' number-one draft choice in 1966, Jerry was a man who could become genuinely ornery during a game. His over-all devotion to football, plus his temperament, made him perfectly suited for his job. Quiet and retiring off the field, Jerry was known for his toughness and his refusal to buckle in game situations.

DEFENSIVE TACKLE: Jim Kanicki, age twenty-eight, 6' 4", 270 pounds. Towering over Jerry Shay, his partner, Jim was opening the season for us after seeing limited exhibition action because of a pulled hamstring muscle. A tower of physical strength, with Charles Atlas biceps and the power to bench-press nearly 500 pounds, Jim came to the Giants from Cleveland with a reputation for not giving it everything he had all the time. His greatest game probably came during his rookie year in 1964, when he mercilessly manhandled the Baltimore Colts' Jim Parker—considered by many to be the greatest offensive lineman of all time—in the NFL Championship game. Happy with life in Cleveland, Jim had missed part of the sixty-nine season owing to a broken leg and came to New York without much enthusiasm. This was to change as the season progressed, but he opened the year as a question mark—a veteran with imposing muscular power and untapped potential but still recovering from his damaged hamstring.

DEFENSIVE END: Bob Lurtsema, age twenty-eight, 6' 6", 250 pounds. "Lurts" was one of the resident zanies of the club. A graduate engineer and part-time inventor (with several patents pending), he more than offset this serious side with constant joking around the locker room. A four-year man, he was the most veteran of our starting linemen and to his job he brought strength, smartness, modest speed, a leadership quality (he was the unanimous choice as the team's Players Association representative) and tremendous hands, which he used for slapping and shoving around offensive linemen. "Lurts" had been badly misunderstood under the Sherman regime and his full potential had never been tapped. With the loss of Wesley Grant, he had made the difficult switch from defensive end to defensive tackle with great alacrity and was set to operate as a fine leader of the front four.

DEFENSIVE END: Fred Dryer, age twenty-four, 6′ 6″, 228 pounds. In many ways, "Fearless" was the embodiment of the football player of the seventies. Free-spirited, thanks in the main to his great ability as a pass rusher. Lighter than many defensive ends (although I can name more top-flight defensive linemen in the NFL today who weigh *under* 240 pounds than over). Fred's quickness was breath-taking. He is the only man I've ever seen that good offensive linemen have whiffed on completely—never so much as touched him as he zoomed past and into their backfield! A devotee of long hair, hard rock and VW buses, Fred was in the vanguard of a refreshing new wave of the future that was pouring over pro football. No man on the Giants outhustled Dryer at any time.

RIGHT LINEBACKER: Matt Hazeltine, age thirty-seven, 6′ 1″, 220 pounds. An All-Pro linebacker with impeccable credentials especially effective on pass coverage. He brought immeasurable poise and understanding to our linebacking corps. Exceptionally bright and articulate and we've already mentioned Matt's return from a lucrative business career for one more year of football. He shared an apartment with Fred Dryer for the season, and a certain amount of Fred's life-style had its effect. I can remember seeing Matt and Fred—thirteen years apart in age—having dinner at Joe Morrison's restaurant around midseason. Both were wearing

T-shirts and bell-bottom Levis. Who said there was a generation gap in pro football? When I'd played against Matt and the 49ers regularly during my Viking years, I was convinced that there was no better linebacker anywhere.

LEFT-SIDE LINEBACKER: Ralph Heck, age twenty-nine, 6′ 1″, 230 pounds. An official team prankster, Ralph had a legendary reputation for never sleeping, training on endless packs of cigarettes and prodigious quantities of Scotch and generally raising hell throughout the season. A really fun guy, Ralph kept the training camp in turmoil with his practical jokes, especially in company with Greg Larson. Of course training-camp monkey business is a basic part of pro football, and Ralph's hazing of the rookies was brilliantly diabolical. Had he been on the Vikings during my tenure there, he would have been a ringleader in our annual trick on the rookies after the final cuts had been made and the forty-man lineup was settled. With a great sense of relief evident in our few remaining youngsters, I'd go to their rooms and give them the following story: Word had passed through the dorm that Van Brocklin was on his way back from a nearby saloon, drunk and surly. He was apt to make a surprise bed check, so I advised them to get into bed early, turn out their lights and leave their doors unlocked so Dutch, in the terrible mood he was in, could gain easy entry. Once these poor guys were bedded down, the veterans would burst in on them and douse them with wastebaskets full of cold water. Ralph would have liked that. When he wasn't raising hell, Ralph was playing a great game of football. A smart, gutsy, eight-year veteran of the wars at Philadelphia and Atlanta before coming to the Giants, Ralph played middle linebacker for us in 1969 and was assigned again as the defensive signal caller. Not large for his position, he brought tremendous experience and nerve to the game and, with Matt Hazeltine, flanked our young middle linebacker, Jim Files, with a pair of the savviest players in the business.

MIDDLE LINEBACKER: Jim Files, age twenty-two, 6′ 4″, 240 pounds. Our only rookie starter, this quiet, red-headed kid from Fort Smith, Arkansas, somehow made it through training camp while being shown some of Manhattan's night life by his self-appointed tour guide, Ralph Heck. A former high school quarterback and Oklahoma U. linebacker, Jim contributed four great assets to his position—speed, coordination, strength and intelligence—traits that may make him one of the greatest linebackers in history. He had already gotten high grades for his pass coverage but was looking to his older cohorts, Heck and Hazeltine, to show him the way to more effective defense against the run.

RIGHT CORNERBACK: Willie Williams, age twenty-seven, 6′ 0″, 190 pounds. Very likely the finest all-around athlete on the team, Willie left the Giants in 1966 to play with the Oakland Raiders. After returning to New York, he led the league in interceptions in 1968 and played in the 1969 Pro Bowl. Willie would rather play golf than eat, literally, and during the lunch break in two-session practice days can be found at the nearest driving range, A fine passer and punter, Willie and his close friends Spider Lockhart and Scott Eaton also play basketball for hours on end. Willie was one of the best deep pass defenders in the league and, with Spider and Scott, made up a secondary that was the single strongest entity on our entire team.

FREE SAFETY: Spider Lockhart, age twenty-seven, 6′ 2″, 175 pounds. Spider had everything to qualify him as the best free safety in the game—speed, sure hands, brains, guts, tackling ability, a fierce competitive spirit—you name it; it belonged to Spider. In addition to his truly All-Star, All-Pro talents, which don't have to be belabored here, Spider also qualified, without serious competition, as the Giants' best-dressed man.

LEFT CORNERBACK: Scott Eaton, age twenty-five, 6′ 3″, 205 pounds. A basketball player at Oregon, Scott came to the Giants in 1967 as a free agent who'd never played college football. A fine athlete, Scott was viewed as one of the best young secondary men in the game, but his vulnerability to injury had consistently prevented him from reaching his potential.

STRONG SAFETY: Tommy Longo, age twenty-six, 6′ 1″, 205 pounds. A tough, former Notre Damer from New Jersey, Tommy was on the spot. Bruce Maher, a superb ten-year veteran from Detroit, was expected to give us great strength at the position, but he had a serious personality conflict with one of the coaches and simply was not invited back to camp in 1970. With Bruce gone, Tommy had been thrust into the strong safety spot even though he'd never played the position before and to make matters worse, had been injured for much of the exhibition season. His spirit notwithstanding, Tommy's novice status at this key position left us with a serious question mark in our defense.

SPECIALISTS, KEY RESERVES

PLACE KICKER: Pete Gogolak, age twenty-eight, 6′ 1″, 190 pounds. One of the first soccer-style kickers in pro football, Pete became a key figure in the old AFL-NFL warfare when he jumped, amid great furor, from the Buffalo Bills to the New York Giants. A premier-place kicker, surely as good as any in the league.

PUNTER: Bill Johnson, age twenty-seven, 6′ 2″, 205 pounds. Bill had come to us from the Orlando Panthers, a team that gained fame by hiring pro football's first lady player. A soft-spoken, sensitive kid who's towering left-footed kicks during the exhibition season gave us confidence that our punting would be a strong point of our game.

KEY RESERVES

Running back, Joe Morrison, age thirty-three, 6′ 1″, 212 pounds (what more can be said about Joe?).

Running back, Bobby Duhon, age twenty-four, 6′ 0″, 195 pounds, a fine runner who like Joe, had been beaten out of the starting halfback's job by Ron Johnson. We expected him to contribute as the number-one reserve for Johnson and a key kickoff return man. A complete team player, Bobby could be counted on to be in the middle of any fight and yelling louder on the sidelines than any other two guys. He entered each game as the Giants' Defender, prepared to uphold the honor of the team, alone if necessary. A quarterback at Tulane, Bobby was within a whisker of being as good as Johnson and would generate several key plays during the season. His romance with Tucker Frederickson's beautiful sister Mary Ann was to culminate in marriage a few months later.

Aaron Thomas, age thirty-two, 6′ 3″, 215 pounds, had come out of retirement after the brokerage firm he had been working for, Goodbody & Company, had hit hard times. Aaron, a veteran, had lost some of his speed, but his experience at running pass patterns made him a valuable utility receiver.

Joe Green, age twenty-three, 5′ 11″, 185 pounds, a terror from Bowling Green who operated as a sort of general harasser of the enemy on all special teams and as a backup for Spider Lockhart.

Charlie Harper, age twenty-six, 5′ 11″, 250 pounds, an offensive lineman who was to become a key reserve. A smart, agile player, Charlie had the unique ability to operate at either guard or tackle (the positions require completely different moves and most men find switching from one to the other nearly impossible).

Although they had no direct bearing on the fortunes of our team, the cast of characters in our locker room were as deeply involved with us as anybody who threw a block or a football. While our trainers, John Dzeigiel and John Johnson, were fine professionals who did yeoman service in keeping all of us in repair, "Subway Sid" Moret, our equipment manager, and Pete Privette, our clubhouse attendant, did more than their share to keep us in stitches. Sid was the ultimate native New Yorker, complete with the tough, loud talk, unsolicited opinions on all subjects, and the skill to turn a buck on practically everything inside the locker room. His nickname apparently stems from his repeated efforts to initiate young Giant players to the mysteries of the New York subway system. Sid is a great pinup man, forsaking Playboy Bunnies, etc., in favor of slogans, bad poems and strident urgings hung on the walls and inside lockers to inspire us to greater deeds on the field. One of Sid's prime moments comes each year at training camp, where he supervises the small regiment of boys who act as ball retrievers for the team, and the one sound that will stay with me always as a reminder of my years with the Giants is the gravelly, harsh accent of "Subway Sid" Moret echoing over the practice field admonishing his boys to "move with a purpose!"

Outside of Pete Sheehy, Pete Privette has attended the Yankee Stadium locker room longer than any man can remember. In the summer he labors for the Yankees, in the fall for the Giants, polishing shoes, providing coffee and soft drinks and doing minor chores for the players. Each team member must pay three dollars in dues per week to Pete, who collects each Tuesday, come hell or high water. Coffee and soft drinks, which we accuse Pete of getting free, cost us twenty cents apiece. Nobody escapes from Pete and his collections. What's more, he carries on a thriving business in selling autographed footballs (which he buys for six dollars and sells for nine). Each morning the table in the center of the locker room is crowded with balls awaiting our signatures, and little Pete is standing at the door, herding us toward the signing process. There is a limit to the time each man likes to sign his own name and certain numbers of us have been known to skip the occasional ball—like every other one, if Pete isn't paying attention—despite his constant warning, "OK, you guys, sign them balls and no skippies! You heard me, No skippies!" Pete's particular encounter with destiny came in 1964, when he suggested a play to Allie Sherman. Just before half time Pete volunteered that all the fastest men be put on the field at once and sent out for a pass in kind of a mad scattershot play. As it turned out, cornerback Erich Barnes caught the ball and scored a touchdown. Pete hasn't been the same since, and if anything, the whole thing encouraged him in his rapid-fire joke making and sloganeering—an effort that results in such gems as "Fran the scram, he ran and ran."

There we were, a thin red, white and blue line, ready to face fourteen NFL teams in what we had hoped would be a journey to the first really successful season since 1964. First came the Bears.

Game One
GIANTS VS. CHICAGO BEARS
Yankee Stadium, New York City
Saturday evening, September 19, 1970
Giants record: 0–0

It was a little strange, driving down to the Stadium from our rented house in Greenwich, Connecticut. For years it had been a tradition that the Giants spend the night before home game at the Doral Hotel on Park Avenue, but Alex had changed that in favor of letting the guys stay with their families. Those little rituals that pervade all sports have intangible effects, and in this particular case it made no difference to me. Mind you, I wasn't about to change my own special, pre-game routine—laced with a certain amount of superstition, I'll admit—just because we weren't bunking in at the Doral anymore.

Cruising along the parkways leading toward the Bronx, I reflected on the strengths and weaknesses of the two teams and became even more convinced we could whip the Bears. Admittedly, we had ten new starters, some old men, some rookies, some rejects from other teams, and a number of guys with unproven capabilities. What's more, Scott Eaton would not start. A nagging injury would sideline him in favor of Kenny Parker, a Fordham kid who'd spent two years on our taxi squad. Kenny was a gutsy guy who wouldn't let being beaten on a pass play bother him (and that's critical, because a cornerback must mentally toughen himself to the inevitability of being beaten and looking like a complete incompetent in front of the entire world), but suddenly our secondary, filled with four excellent veterans last year, was depleted to veterans Lockhart and Williams aided by a pair of earnest but inexperienced youngsters. As a gesture to their years of service, Alex planned to open with Joe Morrison at half back and Aaron Thomas at tight end. Then there was Bob Lurtsema, trying his first game at defensive end, and thirty-seven-year-old Matt Hazeltine, about to start his first game in two years, beside rookie Jim Files.

We thought we had the making of a good team, but the book on us around the league said we were a patchwork collection of question marks. The smart money said we were heading for another mediocre season. But the sense of individual looseness that leads to unity was present on the Giants for the first time in many seasons and we knew we were better than a cursory examination of our roster indicated. This Giant team was different. It sounds banal beyond belief to describe the Giants as happy, but that was our essential strength as we gathered at the stadium to face the Bears.

The Bears appeared to be in a heap of trouble. They'd won but one game the year before, and a knee injury to the all-time star Gale Sayers, coupled with uncertain play by quarterbacks Jack Concannon and Bob Douglass, had blunted their offense. Trades in the off season had given them LeRoy Caffey, who in concert with Doug Buffone and the incomparable Dick Butkus, provided the Bears with as strong a linebacking corps as there was in football. The defensive front four was solid, but their secondary was weak and we figured we could pass effectively against them. Sayers was entering the game still trying to regain full strength in his knee, and Butkus was also laboring with a strained knee.

Jack Concannon was supposed to start and that made our defense happy. Possessing a strong arm and good manuever-ability (let's not call him a "scrambler"), Jack had failed to prove himself as a consistent frontline quarterback after seven years in the league. Although he'd played some superb individual games, his primary problem was passing accuracy and insufficient experience to probe defenses with steady, short-pass completions. With the Bears' running game hampered by Sayers' troubles, we thought we could keep them from scoring, while it seemed that we could penetrate their defense *if* Butkus & Company could be neutralized. You cannot play around a superlative operator like Dick. He must be isolated on each play, either by screening or blocking, because he is the kind of player who will range all over the field to destroy offenses. Great players make great plays. They are not quiet workmen who labor diligently but unspectacularly week in and week out; they are men who crush teams single-handedly, change the course of games, demoralize the enemy and inspire their cohorts with brilliant, sometimes superhuman, actions. Great plays, as I said, come from great players like Butkus. Butkus has been painted as a dumb football animal, but nothing is further from the truth. He is enormously bright, with a nearly perfect football temperament, and he never, ever, gives up. His concentration is uncanny. On his last play of the last 1969 game, with Chicago losing 20–3 and headed for their worst season in history, Butkus was playing just as hard as he had in the opener. He is that kind of man and in order to beat the Bears he and his partners, Caffey and Buffone, who are very nearly as good, had to be dealt with by disciplined passing that would put them man to man on faster backs and flankers, and by hard blocking by our offensive line that would establish our running game.

I arrived at the stadium about four fifteen and the place

was deserted, except for a few cops who lounged near the entrances and a small collection of concessionaires who were beginning to organize their substantial tonnage of programs, pillows, banners and other oddments that would be gobbled up by the sellout crowd that evening. I went into the locker room and spent some time going over the key plays we planned to use. That was probably a mistake. You can think too much about a game plan (which, by the way, is an overworked designation, the implication being that a quarterback operates like a dancer, unfolding his game in a series of precise maneuvers, as if each last step of the entire offensive team had been laid out by a choreographer. That is nonsense. A game plan sets out to penetrate certain presumed weaknesses in an opposing team's defense, but it is at best a general concept, subject to momentary change and adjustment throughout the contest).

I do it the same way every week of the season. I guess you could call it a ritual, although that implies that I am invoking some mystical power by my actions. I don't think that's the case, but routines that athletes develop all fill some indefinable need, and I suppose mine are no exception. Anyway, it's my habit to get partially dressed long before the game and kind of unwind my way to the kickoff. First I tape my ankles, put on my hip pads and my solid-blue Giant socks with the white athletic socks over them. Then I slide into my game pants and my T-shirt and just lounge around the locker room, reading the program and chatting with other players who've arrived early. About an hour before kickoff I wander back into the little medical office to carry on what I call my "brain trust" session with our team doctors, Rudi Bono and Tony Pisani. Rudi and Tony are a pair of gifted general surgeons who've served the Giants' ailments for years. Rudi is small and intense and Tony is a tall, heavy-set man who towers over his colleague. They are tremendously intelligent, genial men and our conversations range over a variety of subjects—normally excluding football. The intent is to relax me and distract my thinking from the game as a sort of sedative before the action begins. I have come to value these sessions with Rudi and Tony as critical to my state of mind before a game, and their elimination would oblige me to make some serious adjustments in my mental countdown procedures. Although politics or current events often dominate our talks, I can remember on that particular occasion that I remarked to them that no matter how long I play, there's nothing like the opening game of the season. It brings on a special kind of tenseness and anticipation that is lacking even in the key games that come later in the year. Each September it's a *new* team, unproved, untested and unbeaten, and the more times you wait for the first whistle of the year to sound, the more tantalizing the moment becomes.

I used to go out on the field early with the punters and place kickers to loosen up, but since we began to win late in the 1969 season I'd stopped that and wasn't about to resume. You can write that one off to pure superstition.

Beating the Bears was going to be easier than we thought. Although I firmly believe that a running game must be established before victory can be guaranteed, we became fascinated with passing against the Bears. In the first quarter I faked a draw play, then tossed a quick screen pass to Ron Johnson and he zoomed down the sideline for an easy touchdown. It was almost too easy. You've got to remember that a passing game is a great deal harder than it looks, especially on the offensive linemen. When pass blocking, they're taking a tremendous amount of punishment from the defense and this is both tiring and frustrating to them. This strain on them, plus the miles of running by the ends and backs, can take the steam out of an offense rather quickly. In fact, if a team throws more than twenty-five to thirty passes per game, you can be reasonably sure they're in a heap of trouble.

Gogolak kicked off to Cecil Turner, one of the most feared return men in the business. But we had our special teams, the Giants' new secret weapon! Turner took the ball near the goal line and embarked on a run that might have unfolded in a game of touch. He made several minor course changes on the way to our goal line and breezed to a touchdown without a Giant getting within shouting distance. Damn! The blasted special teams! We went back to work and continued to fling the ball around the field with great success. Up and down we thundered, completing passes and boring sizable holes up the middle. When the first half ended we'd gained 300 yards in total offense. But we only had 10 points on the scoreboard.

At half time, things looked great. Some of the guys were cheered because Butkus' knee had gotten so bad that he'd sat out the final three minutes, but I tried to assure them the old warhorse would be back for the second half if he had to play in an iron lung. In football you keep doing something until the opposition won't let you do it anymore. We'd passed them silly in the opening thirty minutes and it stood to reason they weren't going to give up another 300 yards in the second two quarters. But I got pass-happy and ignored our running game until it was too late.

As I said, you can't expect to gain 300 yards every half, and the Bears toughened after the third quarter opened. Then they took our passing game away. Butkus was everywhere, looking more like Peg Leg Pete, dragging his bad limb behind him but roving all over the field making powerful tackles, pouncing on receivers and knocking pass plays askew. We lost momentum. We began to miss third down plays. Passes were dropped, blocks were missed. I threw some bad balls. At this point a strange transfer of spirit took place. The Bears had been knocked around the field and now they were stopping us. Confidence in their secondary soared and they began to stiffen. Their offense, seeing that we couldn't move, gained enthusiasm and scored again to lead, 14–10. That brought them further reinforcement and before we could do anything about it, the entire initiative had been transferred to the Bears.

They gambled. We'd stopped them on their 45 yard line, and Bobby Joe Green dropped back to punt. Bobby had been a quarterback in high school and had been known to pass from this formation but not with his team nursing a 4-point lead inside their own territory. Not much. We rushed nine men while wide receiver Bob Wallace eased into the flat and caught a toss from Green. He was finally stopped on our 20, but they went into score again. *Damn, damn, damn!* those special teams! We cussed and kicked turf up and down the sidelines. Frustration! Burned twice for two cheap touchdowns by what we thought would be a new strength of the Giants. Grumbling among ourselves, unsure of our strategy, hopelessly tardy in establishing a ground game, we trudged back on the field and somehow managed to get another field goal to trail 21–13.

We were coming apart at the seams, but we knew we were better than the Bears and we still had a chance to prove it. Then, on a third-down pass play, Willie Holman, the Bears 6′ 4″ defensive tackle, laid a forearm across my head that about knocked me silly. It wasn't a cheap shot; his arm simply caught me square and I went down in a fog. I didn't lose consciousness, but I was fuzzy—probably fuzzier than

I thought. I continued to play and Gogolak edged us closer with his third field goal of the game. The clock was counting off the final minutes of the fourth quarter; we had one more crack at winning. The ball was on our 20 and we needed short yardage for the first down. I called our old standby "13 pass, A-option," a play that had worked so well for us in 1969 I'd become almost embarrassed to use it anymore. It was exquisitely simple. Both backs would curl out of the backfield, with the fullback heading toward the strong-side linebacker and the halfback taking on the weak-side linebacker. Normally the middle linebacker moves to the strong side while our halfback fakes either inside or outside, then cuts into the open for an easy completion. In 1969, with Joe Morrison running the play, we completed over 90 per cent of our passes with that call and it *had* to work this time.

Joe was at halfback; Tucker Frederickson was playing fullback. As I dropped back, I saw the great bulk that was Butkus pause, detect a passing play, step backward tentatively, then edge to his left, toward the strong side. Perfect! That left Joe man on man on Doug Buffone. I spotted Morrison over the welter of churning linemen and could see he had Buffone beat. I figured Joe was going to make his cut inside and flung the ball away. As it was streaking through the air, Joe made a perfect move, giving a little head fake and darting outside—away from the ball! This left Buffone dead center, right on target, and the ball thumped against his chest for one of the most humiliating interceptions of my career. It looked as if I had thrown the blasted thing right at him! Joe and I had been executing that play perfectly for over a year. I'd never read his cut wrong before. If I'd been able to think quickly I know I'd have waited that split second to catch Joe's final move and would have completed the pass as I'd done so many times before.

That cut it. The Bears took a field goal that put them in front 24–16 and we'd lost the opener. It hurt. We needed the victory to prove to ourselves that our uncertain alliance of new and old players would do the job, and a series of unexpected errors had cost us the game. Elaine and I dropped by Tucker Frederickson's apartment for a while, then had a solemn dinner at Dewey Wong's, a little Chinese place I favor in Manhattan. On the way home to Greenwich, along the same parkways I'd driven down with so much hope a few hours earlier, I could only think of the screw-ups and how the season was off on the wrong foot again. Then, on the other hand, there had been the locker room after the game. The guys were sore. We were outraged at ourselves for blowing the thing to a team we should have beaten. But that was good. We were animated about our anger, involved with one another. It meant we cared.

Game Two
GIANTS VS. DALLAS COWBOYS
Cotton Bowl, Dallas
Sunday afternoon, September 27, 1970
Giants record: 0–1

The Dallas Cowboys were hardly a together team. For the first time since their winless debut in 1960, the fans were really giving them some heat. These same supporters had been among the most frenzied in the NFL, but a pair of championship losses to Green Bay in 1966 and 1967, coupled with two shocking drubbings at the hands of the underdog Cleveland Browns in the sixty-eight and sixty-nine

Eastern Conference title game, had left their supporters (and detractors as well) howling that the Cowboys couldn't win the big ones. For the first time since he had arrived in Dallas, Tom Landry, the team's gifted and creative coach, was under attack. Bob Hayes had played out his option and was publicly talking about being traded. Don Meredith, a fixture at quarterback and a favorite hero-villain for the Dallas fans, had left the team, making little secret that he didn't like Landry. Unconfirmed rumors of dissension and feuding (some of it racial) within the team swept through the league. Craig Morton, a rather enigmatic, introverted Californian, was having trouble assuming a leadership role at quarterback, which, coupled with injuries that hampered his passing, was defusing an otherwise powerful offense.

The Cowboys, although as abundant with talent, from backfield to bench, as any other team in football, were having troubles and we felt they could be had. Their exhibition season had been awful and their first game against the demoralized Philadelphia Eagles netted them a narrow, unconvincing victory. You cannot simply presume victory with a team as physically powerful and experienced as the Cowboys, no matter how troubled they might be. I personally believe the team has the best scouting and coaching techniques in the game, and their first-forty men represent a cornucopia of athletic skill. Their starting twenty-two, with people like Bob Lilly, who may very well be the greatest defensive lineman in the history of football, offensive tackle Ralph Neely, guard John Niland, linebackers Lee Roy Jordan and Chuck Howley, secondary men like Cornell Green, Mel Renfro and Herb Adderley, plus Jethro Pugh, Hayes, etc., boggles the mind for its sheer concentration of ability. Yet they were victims of that strange malaise that overcomes teams and forces their confidence to falter and to make them more vulnerable than any enemy could reasonably expect.

You never beat a great team like the Cowboys by taking chances. Gambles can mean mistakes, and the one way they will thump you into tiny pieces is by giving them mistakes like interceptions and fumbles that they turn into cheap touchdowns. Minimizing mistakes is critical in any game, but with a lesser team it is not quite so important. After all, they might reciprocate with an even worse mistake and nullify whatever break you might have given them. Not so with the Cowboys, especially on the familiar, windswept, artificial turf of the Cotton Bowl. I expected it to be hot, which it was not. I expected it to be windy, which it was. I expected the synthetic turf, which the Giants had played on only once before, to be unresilient and rather slippery. It was.

We were going to beat them by playing it cool, operating with a tightly disciplined short-passing game that would lead to ball control. Dallas is known to "flex" its defensive front four, depending on whether the situation indicates pass or run. For example, on the first down, when a run is likely, two of the four will set themselves a few feet back from the line of scrimmage to give themselves better pursuit angles on the runners. On passing downs, they will pack up tight against the line to rush the quarterback. Our plan was hardly complicated—to run when they were set for the pass, to pass when they "flexed." For the first half it worked. We moved the ball carefully but effectively and got ourselves a touchdown while holding the Cowboys to a field goal.

In the locker room at half time we were noisy and animated, pleased with our play and with the score. In the confusion the coaches and I discussed injecting a trick play into the opening of the second half—a play designed to add a blitzkreig touchdown and presumably put the game out of reach for the sagging Dallas offense. Morton had been benched in favor of Roger Staubach, a solid quarterback who simply lacked experience to propel the Cowboys to any meaningful point totals. Seven quick points could be decisive against the Cowboys.

The plan was this: On the first offensive play of the second half, I was to call what we had referred to all week as the "streak pass." We had tried it a number of times in practice and it had worked like a charm—a sure touchdown every time. *The secret play!* Frank Merriwell strikes again! It was supposed to work like this: We set up in a double-wing formation, with the flanker back (in this particular case, Rich Houston, because of his superior speed) setting up on the strong side and going in motion. On the snap, Ron Johnson was to head downfield, pulling the strong safety with him and opening the center for Houston who was "streaking" (get it?) in diagonally from right to left across the field. From there all I had to do was fling the ball 30 yards downfield into the waiting arms of Rich, who would sprint into the end zone unscathed. It had to work, they argued, and it would put us in a powerful position for the final half.

I was against it. Our ball control had worked well for us for the first two quarters and I couldn't see where taking a wild gamble like this could do anything but hurt us. You don't beat a team like Dallas by taking risks, I argued. It was a fact that the longer we could keep them at bay, the less a factor their defense would become. The pressure would shift to their offense, thereby leaving them vulnerable for a game-breaking error. What's more, we had the brisk Cotton Bowl breeze in our faces during the third quarter, which might hamper the streak pass, but more important, we would leave them to contend with the wind in the final period. Then we could play it cozy, keeping them deep in their territory with punts and relying on the head wind to impede their field goals and long passes. The dispute spilled out onto the sidelines for the opening of the second half, when we kicked off to Dallas.

They moved the ball upfield, then bogged down inside the 50 and tried a field goal. The pass from center was off target, and the holder, Dan Reeves, was forced to run before being downed on our 43 yard line. We had the ball. *The streak pass!* This time it came to me as an order and I jogged onto the field grumbling about the decision. I called the play and I waited for the snap from Greg Larson, I watched Houston start into motion and listened to the breeze float my signals up into the great bowl that surrounded us. The ball was in my hands and the thumps and grunts of the linemen filled my ears as I dropped back, curling to my right, scanning Houston and Johnson as they angled downfield. Rich had his man, Herb Adderly, beaten by five yards. At the last second I arced the ball deep downfield in his direction and watched in horror as the Cowboy's young free safety, Cliff Harris, resisted Ron's lure and sped into the corner of the play. He snared the ball at full gait and sprinted upfield with a shocked, angry Giant team huffing in pursuit. He was downed on our ten yard line, where Staubach was to strike for a touchdown to tie the score. I stomped off the field, furious with myself for throwing a bad ball (let's make one thing clear: There is virtually no excuse, *ever,* for a quarterback to throw an interception, and don't ever forget it. One always has the option of eating the ball, throwing it away or wonder of wonders, passing it more accurately, and guys who blame their receivers, etc., are guilty of a terrible cop-out) and furious with myself for not making my own decisions.

That was it. The momentum floated away from us on that warm Dallas breeze and we were never really in the game again. I threw another interception on the next series of downs and Dallas had another score handed to them. We had broken the cardinal rule for upsetting great football teams; we had given them cheap touchdowns—a favor they refused to return—and from there on in their powerful defense had us at bay and we went down 28–10.

Although there was very little recrimination or complaining on the airplane back to New York, I was bothered by the confusion over the streak pass. For two straight weeks we had been dealing with a collection of enthusiastic, involved experts, each of whom had a great deal to offer but answered to no one. Early Tuesday morning I met with Alex in his office. "Listen, Alex, you know that everybody is raising hell about the Dallas thing," I said. "And you know that it's you and I they're blaming. I've been trying to please everybody—you, Ken, Joe, Y. A., Rosie, all the guys—but that just doesn't work. I need all the help I can get during the week and I appreciate what they have to offer, but on Sunday afternoon it's you and me—we're the guys holding the bag. And, Alex, if you and I are going to take the brunt for the mistakes, you and I better damn well at least have the responsibility for making those mistakes."

Alex agreed instantly. At first a few of the coaches took Alex's announcement that he and I would make final decisions on sideline strategy as a personal rebuff, but that wasn't the case and they soon realized it. Alex took charge of the situation in fine fashion and it helped to clear the air before we faced New Orleans. At least if we did the unthinkable and lost to the Saints, they'd know exactly whom to blame.

Game Three
GIANTS VS. NEW ORLEANS SAINTS
Sugar Bowl, New Orleans
Sunday afternoon, October 4, 1970
Giants record: 0–2

We had New Orleans figured as a terrible team. They were in a great state of flux, with tremendous pressures being placed on their players and their coach, Tom Fears (who was to be fired a short time later), by a management that didn't seem to understand quite what it was doing and by an angry collection of fans. The Saints had a pretty solid defense, with a front four who were strong against the run, and a young, mobile secondary, but their offense was in terrible shape. Billy Kilmer, who had solid skills at quarterback but couldn't seem to get it all together with the Saints, was being alternated with Edd Hargett, a second-year man. Their best runner, Andy Livingston, was out for the season with an injury and they had but one quality receiver in tight end Dave Parks. What's more, the team was mentally unhinged enough to give up cheap touchdowns. The week before they had held the Vikings' offense at bay for much of the game but lost when Minnesota blocked a pair of punts and converted them into easy touchdowns. When it was all over, we could look back and judge New Orleans as easily the worst team we'd played all year. But we still lost.

Man, did we move the ball. The Saints' defense wasn't as strong as we had expected and we jumped to a 3–0 lead early in the game. Then we powered down the field again and got a first down on the 1-foot line. I handed the ball to Ron

Johnson and he burrowed his way in for the touchdown. But the officials said he failed to make it and placed the ball on the 1-inch line. Ron went in a second time. Again, the referees said no. (Both plays resulted unquestionably in touchdowns, the game films would reveal later.) They held on fourth down and we left the field feeling cheated.

Most teams play harder against New York representatives in any sport, and New Orleans was no exception. They were trying their best, in spite of the heavy booing that filled the aging Sugar Bowl. Happily, the crowd was on the Saints, not us, so we went to work again, trying to boost the score against a team we knew we could whip. We'd been practicing a play where I faked a handoff to Ron, then made a quick throw to Clifton down the sidelines. We completed it to their 5 yard line, but the officials called it back. Charlie Harper was filling in for Pete Case, who'd hurt his ankle earlier, and the men in the striped shirts said he'd been holding. (Again, the game films gave no evidence whatsoever that Charlie had committed the violation.) A short time later Clifton took another long pass to set us up on their 25 yard line, but that too was nullified. The officials said McNeil had lined up too far back, meaning we did not have seven men on the line of scrimmage. This is such a discretionary situation, involving the judgment of both the player and the line judge (both of whom may think differently), that a warning is usually issued before a flag is thrown. Not so this time, and once again we were dragged, kicking and yelling, out of New Orleans territory.

The Saints got a touchdown and a second field goal in the second half and suddenly the game was ticking away with us behind 13–10. We were still sailing smoothly up and down the field but could not score. Pete Gogolak had missed a couple of field goals and I'd missed a few passes and we'd had a couple of fumbles. That's all it takes, plus the bad calls, to convert 400 yards of offense into a measly 10 points. With time running out, we mounted another strong drive and got to their 10 yard line. On third down I called "Sweep 27, B diagonal," in which I fake a handoff to Ron, who's sweeping right, then toss to Tucker Frederickson, who had moved outside the tight end, in this particular case, Aaron Thomas. But John Brewer, the Saints' outside linebacker, had broken off Aaron's block and had Tucker covered. With the Saints' rugged pair of tackles, Dave Rowe and Mike Tilleman, in hot pursuit, I scrambled toward the left sidelines and sighted Aaron racing into the end zone. He had the Saints' strong safety, Elijah Nevett, beaten by 5 yards and I threw him a ball that had to be a sure touchdown. Aaron gathered it in as he went to his knees, then slid out of the end zone. No touchdown, ruled the official. He'd caught the ball out of bounds, was the claim.

He caught the pass in bounds, I argued, but it was no good. Officials never change their minds and we all know it, but you have to say *something*, hoping somehow it'll force them to use better judgment next time. We missed the score on the fourth down and gave up the ball and the game. Again, the films *clearly* indicate that Aaron Thomas had been in the end zone when he'd caught the ball.

We protested officially to the National League Football Office about the judges and referees, but that would not change the outcome. We'd beaten the Saints everywhere but on the scoreboard and suddenly, horrifyingly, we had played nearly one quarter of our schedule and hadn't won a game. And to make matters worse, two of our losses had come at the hands of Chicago and New Orleans, a pair of the weakest teams in the league. Where did that put us?

Game Four
GIANTS VS. PHILADELPHIA EAGLES
Yankee Stadium, New York City
Sunday afternoon, October 11, 1970
Giants record: 0–3

We returned from New Orleans drained of emotion. It was time for us to begin tearing each other apart and for the natural defense mechanisms to begin operating in a mad fury that would ultimately destroy the team. Logically, the coaches, management and players should have fled to opposite corners and begun flinging insults and recriminations at each other. That's what usually happens when a professional football team blows three games it had a chance of winning—especially when it happens at the beginning of what was supposed to have been a successful season.

That never happened to the New York Giants. Flying up from New Orleans, I sat with Greg Larson and Pete Case. We spent most of the flight reflecting on our plight but never blaming anybody or any group. Other guys were chatting too, quietly trying to put their fingers on what was happening. Somehow, for no really understandable reason, we stayed together. On Tuesday morning we gathered for the first time in the big locker room in Yankee Stadium—that hall of memories for generations of Yankees and Giants—for our meeting that opened weekly practice. Because the Yanks had been finishing out their baseball season, we had been a nomadic team without a real home. For the past three weeks we'd been practicing at little C. W. Post College, each morning struggling through the mire of Long Island Expressway

traffic, to get off at Exit 39 and to work among curious under-
graduates in hopelessly cramped conditions. It didn't feel
right and I've often wondered if the traditionally bad starts
the Giants make each season can't in part be attributed to
their never taking up residency in the stadium until the
third or fourth game. At any rate, we were finally home and
as we shuffled into the meeting we didn't know what to expect. Everybody was there—the scouts, the trainers, even
"Subway Sid," who usually had left by that time of day.

After ten years in pro football I've heard nearly every
speech that can be made and it seemed appropriate for
somebody to stand up and give us the aged "The Season's
Over" routine. It goes something like this: "O.K., you guys,
this season is over. You blew it. Now we're going to have
to build for next year, and the rest of the games are going
to be played to find out which of you dead-beats has enough
desire to stay around for another try," etc., etc. We were
kind of expecting a diatribe like that when Wellington Mara
stood up. Wellington Mara did not talk at his team's meetings as a matter of course. He had been in football for forty-
five years and he'd seen about all of it. He was a quiet,
introverted, conservative man who wasn't given to histrionics,
private or public. But at this point his team was on the rocks
and much of the blame was being pointed in his direction.
After all, it was he who seemingly contradicted logic by pick-
ing Alex as the coach and he practically sold the ranch to
get me. So far neither move had turned his Giants into
winners. The roomful of big men tensed visibly as Wellington
Mara cleared his throat.

"Men, I just have a few things to say this morning," he
said softly. "First of all, you won the game against New
Orleans. You didn't win it on the scoreboard, but you and I
know you beat them and the victory was yours. We've got

a good football team, and somewhere down the line, maybe this year, maybe next year, we are going to win a championship. I can feel it. And when we've got that championship we're going to be able to look back on a game, a day, an event . . . something . . . when it all turned around for us. It may be today, it may be next Sunday against the Eagles, but I know it will happen. Now when that happens and we win that championship, a great many of you will still be here to share that moment. Others, sadly, who don't have that vision will be reading about it in the papers. But no matter what happens or how long it takes for us to reach our goal, we're going to do it together, as a team."

Wellington Mara had made what was without question the finest speech I had ever heard during my career. The effect was instantaneous. Rather than applying more pressure, Wellington Mara had removed pressure. He had recognized the new realities of his sport—that these were not men-children in front of him who could be scared, cajoled and threatened into playing football but were individuals whose primary motivation was internal and highly personalized. Wellington Mara, God bless him, down there in the bowels of Yankee Stadium with the ghosts of Babe Ruth and Steve Owen, tempted by the hard-line customs of the great old days, turned the Giants into winners with a few simple, low-key words. He broke the generation gap.

If Wellington Mara's words helped, so did the world of electronics. Since the year before, the players had been considering the installation of a stereo system in the locker room. The equipment, to be paid for from the kitty built up by the fines collected for being late for practice, etc., was arranged for by Frank Gifford, who worked closely with Westinghouse. By Thursday of that week, the Giants locker room was blaring with the loudest rock music this side of the midtown discothéques. There it was, right in the heart of staid ol' Yankee Stadium, guys getting ready to play football, the game of All-American square jock straps, grooving to the sounds of the Credence Clearwater Revival. It was beautiful. There we were, zip and three in the standings and preparing for our next game with WOR-FM blowing out the walls of Yankee Stadium! It made me recall with amusement my old days at Georgia, when the hours before each game were spent in utter, monastic silence, with each player forced to concentrate completely on himself and his sacred mission in the game. I can remember one session before meeting The Citadel, when we were all huddled in the locker room, supposedly working ourselves into this trance, when somebody started whispering. Wally Butts, our coach, heard the noise and rose up, all 5' 6" of him, and tongue-lashed us for breaking our concentration. He was furious, convinced that the spell was broken and we were rendered helpless.

We beat The Citadel that afternoon 76–0.

All that business of silence and doing penance to some mysterious god of misery and privation may have worked in an older age, but today it is nonsense. We are a looser generation, and tactics that tend to tighten us up before games borders on insanity. The Giants' coaching staff and management were beginning to realize this, and as much as it baffled them, they let the stereo stay—at full volume. When we'd arrive in the morning the system would be playing quiet pop music. We'd change it to hard rock. One morning Wellington Mara came in and amidst the thunder of the Jefferson Airplane I yelled at him, "What do you think Steve Owen would do if he could see this?"

"I have no idea, but I know he's turning over in his grave at this very moment," Wellington called back, a broad smile on his face.

There we were, setting ourselves for Philadelphia with the music, and everything was cool. Even Alex refused to tense up—and he was beginning to catch some real flak from the press and the fans. I can remember him that week, the same ol' Alex, coffee cup in one hand, cigarette in the other, moving around among his team, always pausing to tell one more joke or exchange one more quip with his boys. He never pressed, and somehow, through those days when we knew we had to win one, that it was worth more than having Knute Rockne, The Four Horsemen, all the referees and the Green Berets on our side. We were loose. We were ready for Philadelphia.

On our second play from scrimmage Ron Johnson went 60 yards for a touchdown. Then Gogy got a field goal and Bobby Duhon ran back a punt—the first freaking punt a Giant had run back for a touchdown in what seemed like three hundred years. The Giants fans had barely opened their programs and we had the Eagles 17–0. Then we faltered. On third down I caught Clifton McNeil in their end zone with a 50-yard pass. It was right in his hands. He dropped it. That just happens. All of us drop easy passes, throw nonsensical interceptions, fumble simple handoffs, without any real reason. Nothing can be blamed but the law of averages, I suppose. Then Ron took a pitch-out and went 86 yards for another touchdown. It was called back because Donnie Herrmann moved before the snap. Again, what can you say? It happens to everybody, but suddenly we had a pair of scores voided and the Eagles' spirits perked up.

Although Philadelphia's record concealed the fact, they had a pretty good football team. They had a fine front four buttressed by Tim Rossovich and Gary Pettigrew, a quality quarterback with poise and a strong arm in Norm Snead, fine running power with Tom Woodeshick and instant striking force in the form of ends Ben Hawkins and Harold Jackson. The Eagles' revival came on a pair of Snead-Jackson touchdown passes and suddenly, with the end in sight, we were tied, 23–23. In each of our three losses, we'd led early, only to blow the game in the second half. With minutes remaining it looked as though it might happen again. They were moving the ball, rambling upfield toward what looked like a tie-breaking score and very possibly the winning points. Then we recovered a fumble and the ball was ours at midfield.

I got a little circle pass to Joe Morrison, who had gone in at fullback in order to take advantage of his skill at running pass routes out of the backfield. Joe and that sixth sense of his moved the ball to the Eagle's 35 yard line. With a first down, less than two minutes on the clock and one time-out remaining, I went to the sidelines for a conference with Alex and Joe Walton. They wanted a pass. I wanted to run, feeling that a pass carried with it the following hazards: (1) an interception, (2) being thrown for a loss out of field-goal range, and (3) an incompletion that would stop the clock (we wanted to keep the clock going in order to prevent the Eagles from regaining possession, presuming we scored). On the other hand, a run had the following advantages: (1) any advancement toward the goal would give Gogolak better kicking range, (2) the danger of losing possession would be minimized, (3) the clock would keep running and (4) I thought the Eagles' defense would be looking for the pass.

I called a "Red Right, Sweep 25 trap," which sent Ron Johnson on a sweep to the left side, with Charlie Harper, our left guard, trap-blocking Tim Rossovich. Tim was an ideal candidate for the play. He was extremely fast for a defensive end and when I walked to the line of scrimmage, I could see that he, Pettigrew, Calloway and Mel Tom were split wide, ready to blow in on a *banzai* pass rush. *Beautiful!* I thought to myself. The ball snapped up, Rossovich arrowed ahead and Ron took my handoff and streaked away. Suddenly Charlie Harper was in front of Rossovich, ramming him outside, away from Johnson. Tucker Frederickson plowed into outside linebacker Adrian Young and Ron cut sharply inside while Willie Young sprinted out to get Nate Ramsey, the strong safety. Suddenly the way was clear. Johnson burst into the end zone with his hands high in the air, holding the ball over him in what was to become his trademarked victory signal.

We won it, 30–23. We scored and we led and then we lost that lead and we kept our poise throughout. We had our first victory and we knew others would come. We had a lot of people to thank, not the least of whom were Wellington Mara and the Credence Clearwater Revival.

Game Five
GIANTS VS. BOSTON PATRIOTS
Harvard Stadium, Boston
Sunday afternoon, October 18, 1970
Giants record: 1–3

We arrived in Boston on a dull, snowswept Saturday and few of us ventured outside the Marriott Motel before going to the stadium the next day. I'd never been to Boston before, although Tommy Mason, Rip Hawkins and myself had been drafted by the Patriots before choosing to play with the Vikings. Ironically, the Giants once had a lot of fans from Massachusetts, owing primarily to the years their games had been beamed there on CBS-TV. But that had all changed. The town belonged to the Patriots and we were roundly booed when we jogged into that foreboding old arena called Harvard Stadium.

Like Philadelphia the week before, Boston looked a lot tougher in its game films than its record indicated. Their defense, led by linemen Jim Hunt and Houston Antwine, had raised holy hell with Baltimore and Kansas City the two previous weeks and now it looked as if they might have found a hypo for their floundering offense. Although they had great runners in Carl Garrett and Jim Nance and a superb end in Ron Sellers, the Patriots had felt they needed a big stud at quarterback to get things moving and had paid something akin to the gross national product of Costa Rica to obtain Joe Kapp from the Vikings. Kapp had played briefly the week before against Kansas City, but our game would mark his first appearance in front of the home folks and his first chance to become fully familiar with the Boston system. He represented salvation, or so they thought, and I don't think I can remember when a player got a louder and more enthusiastic welcome than they gave Joe when he was introduced before the game. A lot of guys who never played quarterback will tell you how Joe Kapp isn't very good because his passes wobble. That's bull. Joe Kapp does this much: He leads teams and he usually gets the ball to the man he throws it to, and until they start judging quarterbacks on an artistic point system, like ice skaters, Joe Kapp will remain one helluva professional quarterback.

We played the old numbers game at dinner that night and Joe Morrison maintained his losing streak. Joe had lost in Dallas and New Orleans and we gave him two chances to win, but it just wasn't the night. The numbers game works like this: It's a contest—a game of chance—to see who picks up the dinner check. In this case the participants were Ralph Heck, Bob Lurtsema, Pete Case, Greg Larson, Tucker Frederickson, Joe Morrison and myself. It's my job to pick a number and for the rest of the guys to guess it. The man hitting it on the nose pays. For example, I might pick 200. Then, moving around the table in rotation, each man must guess a number and I must indicate whether he's high or low. When my turn rolls around, I must pick a number one-digit closer to the solution than the next nearest guess—which can easily lose me a bundle. Poor Joe's streak wasn't to be broken that night. He lost the first game and we gave him another chance. He lost again, and after he'd cleared up the seventy-dollar bill we all headed for bed with the wind rattling against the windows of the Marriott, each secretly wondering if Kapp would make the difference.

One could certainly understand Harvard's desire to de-emphasize football, but the locker room situation was ridiculous. We arrived at the massive, gloomy stadium in the midst of a fledgling hurricane and entered a dressing area that would have put a team of pgymies shoulder to shoulder. From there we crunched across three hundred yards of frozen, windswept turf and into a small, dungeonlike cavern in the base of the stadium. I got the impression that I was about to enter some weird, subarctic version of the Roman Coliseum. High walls hugged the playing field, reinforcing the impression of gladiatorial combat, and when it was time to go out for practice, I half-expected to be prodded onto the field by spears wielded by armored centurions.

Practice was insane. The wind lashed around the inside of the stadium with enough turbulance to knock a howitzer shell off course. Some of my passes would be scooped into the air like mini-punts; others would be swatted into the ground by an invisible hand. Pete Gogolak had told me the wind in Harvard Stadium was a legend in the Ivy League, but I had never expected anything this bad. It was the worst I'd ever seen—or imagined. Side-line passes were hopeless and balls flung downfield more than 10 yards could end up anywhere south of Portland, Maine. If we were to pass at all, it would have to be restricted to short flares, swings and screens. This kind of passing attack, coupled with a disciplined, short-yardage running game out of our multiple-formation offense, might do the job, but we were going to have to forget the deep striking power of McNeil and Herrmann unless the wind quit.

I threw 14 passes the entire afternoon, fewer than I'd ever attempted in a game in my professional career, for a mere 103 yards. I threw one touchdown to Clifton to give us a 10–0 half-time lead. (Gogolak had kicked a field goal in the screaming wind—a miraculous feat considering the conditions.) We maintained our shut-out going into the third quarter and felt that if we could get into the fourth period still in the lead the game was ours. The wind was in our face during the third, which meant Ernie "Cowboy" Koy couldn't punt the ball any more than about 15 yards. "Cowboy" had replaced Bill Johnson for the time being and the wind simply tried to shove the ball back down his throat every time he kicked it. However, the fourth quarter would put the wind at our backs and, as in Dallas, might put us in an ideal position to protect a lead.

Kapp was moving the Patriots. With the gale behind him, he'd gotten them to our 35 yard line, then rolled out to pass. His ball arced downfield and toward the arms of Matt Hazeltine. In a magnificent defensive play, Matt nailed Kapp's pass and gave us the ball. Now it was up to us to get a drive underway. We had to move. Otherwise Koy would have to attempt another punt, which very likely would give

Boston excellent field position deep in our territory. We tried two running plays that netted one yard. With third and 9 yards, I called a screen pass to Tucker Frederickson. Tucker gathered in the ball and charged downfield for 10 yards, thanks in part to a perfect block by Greg Larson. "Igor" had left the Eagles game with a strained knee, hadn't practiced all week and had been a doubtful starter, but he'd come back to play a flawless game against Boston. First down!

We tried a similar play moments later and sustained our drive in the teeth of the storm. Finally the clock ran out in the third quarter and we coasted to an easy 16–0 victory—the Giants' first shutout since 1961—125 games earlier. What made us proudest was having played a cool, restrained game, with good ball control and a minimum of mistakes. And most important, for the second week in a row we'd overcome second-half rallies by the opposition.

Game Six
GIANTS VS. ST. LOUIS CARDINALS
Yankee Stadium, New York City
Sunday afternoon, October 25, 1970
Giants record: 2–3

We'd won a pair of games against a couple of bad football teams, they said, and now our day of reckoning would come against the killer Cardinals. After all, they were on a four-game winning binge, were leading the Eastern Conference of the NFC and were brimming over with great stars. They had strong-armed Jim Hart at quarterback, the new running sensation MacArthur Lane, superb receivers

John Gilliam and Jackie Smith, plus Bob Reynolds and Ernie McMillan, perhaps the best brace of offensive tackles in football. Defensively they had the extraordinary Larry Wilson at free safety and Roger Wehrli at cornerback, defensive end Chuck Walker and linebacker Larry Stallings, all top-flight players.

These Cardinals were a football team! How could the upstart, flash-in-the-pan Giants, conquerors of two wounded elephants, hope to handle an aggregation like the Cardinals? Quite well, thank you. Less than a year before, with a weaker collection of players, we had also met the mighty Cardinals as hopeless underdogs. We won that one 49–6.

If I'd been playing golf that Sunday, I'd have knocked in every 20-foot putt I tried. I completed 15 of 18 passes for 5 touchdowns. It was as good a day as I could expect.

One might think the Giants, going up against the division leaders and having to win (if we lost to the Cardinals, they would have been 5 and 1, while we'd have plunged to 2–4 and been out of the race for all intents and purposes), Alex and the coaches might have devised this grand strategy, known as a "game plan"—the football counterpart to the invasion of Europe. This is utter nonsense. "Game plans" are the figment of sportswriters' and television announcers' active imaginations and of some coaches who employ it in the following way: If their team wins, the coach can say, "My quarterback did a great job; he followed the [read "my"] game plan." After a loss he can imply they would have won if the quarterback had followed his so-called "game plan." Alex never used this crutch. Sure we added some new wrinkles each week, but we never developed any formula for beating any given team. We thought we might be able to run inside against St. Louis mainly because they seemed in the past to worry about my "scrambles" and played to keep me in the pocket. But this is the point about the idiocy of the "game plan" hype; we had no idea what St. Louis was going to do, so we could only operate on a few assumptions. I'd probe the inside at the beginning. If they made no effort to shut off the inside running, I'd keep attacking them there. If they blocked the inside, I'd go outside. If they covered my backs coming out of the backfield on pass plays, I'd go to my outside receivers. If the linebackers were dropping back, I'd hit my backs. If they were giving me a hard rush, I'd use screens and draws. Hardly simple, but also hardly a question of creating a rigid plan and sticking to it. As I have said, defense dictates my play calling, and until I see how a defense is responding, I wouldn't attempt to create a "game plan" even if I'd sat in on the opposition's practice session for the past week.

As it turned out, the passing worked to near-perfection. Fortunately, we were able to get Larry Wilson out of position on a couple of plays that went for touchdowns. I'll repeat: Great players make great plays. Larry Wilson is a great player. Therefore, you don't want him to make great plays. One way to do this is not to throw the ball near him. We tried to use a crossing pattern on him, sending Clifton circling deep, with Bob Tucker angling in front of him. I caught Clifton once for a touchdown this way, and Bob Tucker a second time. Bob blossomed as a Giant star that afternoon. The Cardinals were double-covering Ron Johnson in order to cut down his pass receptions and this left Bob open. Before the game was over he'd caught 6 passes for 2 touchdowns and 150 yards. Not bad for a reject from the Boston Patriots and the Philadelphia Eagles.

As in our first five games, we left the field at half time with a lead, in this case a solid 21–10 advantage. But every team that loses in the first half has a chance to win in the second and you can never have too big a safety margin. A quick turn of events and the other guy can rise up and nail you in a tide of emotion and a blizzard of points. Before you know it, you've lost your emotional momentum, your poise and your game. In politics its called peaking too soon before the election. We very nearly did that with the Cardinals. We had them on the ropes, 28–10, and were cruising in for the *coup de grace* when Ron Johnson fumbled on their one-yard line. This left St. Louis with 99 yards to go for a touchdown, which they accomplished with shocking ease. Suddenly the score was 28–17, hardly a runaway, and they had plenty of time to regain the rest of their deficit.

The Cardinals lined up for the kickoff. We were sure they would try an on-side kick and loaded the field with our eleven most sure-handed backs and ends. Their only task was to fall on the football. No fancy running, no anything, except to maintain possession of the ball. But instead of an on-side attempt, St. Louis' Jim Bakken punched out a squib kick that danced crazily over the heads of the nine men we'd stationed up front and wobbled toward Ron Johnson, one of two backs we'd placed deep. Ronnie hesitated for a second, then scooped up the ball and sprinted downfield. In a wink he was clear and drove all the way down to the Cardinals' 20 yard line before being tackled. So much for kickoff plays.

From there Don Herrmann snared a pass to make it 35–17 and give us our third win in a row. Again we'd buckled slightly in the second half but had maintained our cool and our rapidly congealing defense had held on to neutralize the Cardinal's momentum.

That was the week New York discovered Bob Tucker. A few days after the St. Louis game, he was scheduled to appear on Howard Cosell's network radio show and I met him at "21" for a few drinks before his appointment. There was ol'

Bob, who one year previously had been leaning against bars in Pottstown, Pennsylvania, being toasted with fifteen-cent drafts of Schmidt's beer, sitting in the "21" cheek by jowl with the so-called great-and-near-great. One of my very closest friends, Neil Walsh, "The Commander," as we call him (because of his hobby of ocean racing with big power boats), joined us and offered to have Harry, his driver, transport Bob to the ABC studios. But Harry was stuck somewhere in midtown traffic and when it came time for Bob to leave, neither Harry nor any cabs were to be found. However, "The Commander" has never been daunted by such petty troubles. At the curb, he spotted an enormous white Rolls-Royce that belonged to a friend. A quick word with its driver and it was temporarily commandeered for the run to the radio station. The last I saw of Bob Tucker that afternoon—*the* Bob Tucker of Bloomsburg State and the Pottstown Firebirds—he was lounged haughtily in the back seat of that massive white Rolls as it whispered him off toward his interview. Bob Tucker had arrived in New York!

And the Giants were back in town as well.

Game Seven
GIANTS VS. NEW YORK JETS
Shea Stadium, New York City
Sunday afternoon, November 1, 1970
Giants record: 3–3

After our win against St. Louis, Wellington Mara stood in the midst of the locker room jubilation and said to me grimly, "Next week is my game." He was referring to the

New York Jets and how that game, above all others, meant the most to him. They had been his tormentors during the bad years; it had been the Jets whose dazzling success had made the Giants' collapse look even worse than it was. The entire rise of the new sports world at Shea, wherein improbable teams like the Jets and Mets had gaily, almost casually, overwhelmed the competition on the way to world championships, had meant nothing but trouble to Wellington Mara. In contrast, the tenants of Yankee Stadium seemed to be ossifying inside their gray old mausoleum. The sag in the fortunes of the Yankees and Giants was hardly the fault of the new men in Shea, but you couldn't help but understand why Wellington Mara and the rest of us wanted so badly to stomp them.

The bad part of this encounter—our first regular season meeting, and the only one until 1974—was that the Giants had very little to gain and everything to lose. This was because Joe Namath and his two fine running backs, Emerson Boozer and Matt Snell, would miss the game because of injuries. What's more, the Jets had won only one game in six outings, which meant that their season was for all practical purposes a dead issue. They had nothing to lose. If we trounced them, they could fall back on the excuse that it would have been different *if* Namath & Company had played. If they upset us, they could crow that we had been whipped by their second string. On the other hand, a victory by us would bring the claim that we had beaten a crippled team, while a loss, God forbid, would make us the laughing stock of the town. This all meant one thing: They were loose, we were tight.

The New York Jets were a mighty impressive gang of cripples. Everybody will tell you the Jets had a bad season in 1970 because Namath was hurt, but it might be worth noting that ol' Broadway didn't leave the lineup until the

fifth game against Baltimore. At that point they'd won but
once, making it difficult to accept the thesis that Joe's absence
was the sole cause of their troubles. Without Joe, Boozer and
Snell, they were still tough. Al Woodall was a fine young
replacement quarterback and Lee White was filling in effectively as a running back. They had a superb pass-blocking
offensive line that, coupled with magnificent receivers like
Don Maynard (whom the Giants had cut early in his career),
George Sauer, Pete Lammons and Rich Caster gave them a
better offense than might be expected. This same collection
of men several weeks later were to run up 31 points on the
Los Angles Rams and also score enough to beat the mighty
Vikings, which is an indication that they were hardly im-
potent.

I had never met Walt Michaels, the Jets' defensive coach,
but a look at their game films produced a strong admiration
for him. His defensive formations, in which the linemen set
up in gaps and not head to head with their opponents (which
confused blocking assignments), were among the most imag-
inative in the game. His personnel, which included lineman
John Elliott—who I think ranks with players like Bob Lilly
and Alan Page—plus ends Gerry Philbin and Verlon Biggs
and three very intelligent fleet linebackers in Larry Grantham, Al Atkinson and Ralph Baker, gave the Jets one of the
finest defensive units in the game, with special strength to
stop the run. The only weakness could be found in the secondary, where a pair of rookie cornerbacks, Steve Tannen and
Earlie Thomas, could be expected to make mistakes.

Frankly I was nervous. I felt as though I were back in college, about to take the field against our old rivals at Georgia
Tech. I could remember what John Glenn had said when I'd
asked him what it felt like as he was about to lift off on his
three-orbit trip around the earth. He'd said, "I was scared,

but I didn't let my fear interfere with what I had to do." I was trying to operate on the same premise as the Jets game approached. The team spent the night at the Doral in Manhattan before bussing out to Shea—a stadium I'd never been in before. We got there early, which I think did nothing but add to our tenseness and as we walked down the long ramp toward the locker room, I said to "Slugger Shiner," "You know, no matter what stadium you go into—the Cotton Bowl, the Coliseum, Yankee, the high school field in Athens, Georgia—they all smell the same. There's that raw odor in all of them—the odor of combat."

I was farther up for this game than anything since the old Georgia-Georgia Tech blowouts. All the Giants felt the same way and I'm sure the Jets did too. We had a good thing going, with three wins in a row, and we didn't want it to fall apart in the face of a perfectly motivated spoiler like the Jets.

"Trying too hard" is an aged cliché in sports, but there was an element of it in our first-half performance: we were hopelessly stiff and tense. I kept trying to pass deep against Thomas and Tannen and failed to establish consistent drives. Our blocking was ragged and our defense, a gang of guys who'd been so cool for the past few games, simply wasn't hitting. George Nock caught an 8-yard touchdown pass from Woodall in the second quarter while we could do no better than a field goal. We left the field at the half trailing 7–3 and we knew the worst thing we'd done was to give the Jets hope of winning. The press later reported that Alex had blown his stack in the dressing room, that he'd screamed and hollered at us for being flat. This was not true. We went over our offense, decided to return to basic running plays and short passes. Then Alex gathered the team together and gave a brief pep talk of the "Let's go out there and kick their asses all over the field" genre and that was it. We went back to play believing we were more relaxed, but the mental tension was still overwhelming.

Jim Turner kicked a 31-yard field goal and it was 10–3. Trouble. We had to take emotional command. A drive got started with good running and some short square-out passes to Clifton and Bob Tucker. We got to their one-yard line and suddenly it was third down and goal to go. I gave the ball to Tucker Frederickson and he thumped against a wall of green jerseys at the goal line. I leaped into the air with my arms up, signaling touchdown, in some wild hope that my power of suggestion would cause one of the referees to follow suit. Nothing happened, except that Larry Grantham came charging up and asked me (in effect) what in hell I thought I was trying to do by acting like a referee? Larry's tone was something on the dark side of affable and my answer was a rather rude suggestion that it was none of his business. Actually Larry and I get along fine off the field, but on that particular afternoon everybody not on the Giants' bench was an enemy.

I called a "Slant 35" on fourth down, sending Tucker barreling into the line one more time. They were waiting, their powerful front four, and Ivan might as well have been trying to run through the Great Wall of China. He bounced off the big boys and as Steve Tannen began to wrestle him to earth, I shouted, "Lateral!" Tucker spun slightly and flipped the ball back to me under the outstretched arms of Larry Grantham. I started to run to my right, not having heard the whistle, and got thumped by Grantham, Earlie Thomas and Tannen. I was furious. The frustration of not having made the touchdown, coupled with the solid rap the Jets trio had given me, brought me off the ground fighting. Thomas was the first man in sight and I gave him a right-left combination. Fortunately Earlie didn't know that you never lead with your right, and I managed to land a couple of blows in the neighborhood of his helmet. Nothing happened (the most important nonevent was not having broken my throwing hand) and I was dragged off to the sidelines. But the scuffle had triggered a wild melee at the goal line. Both benches emptied and some minor slugging matches took place, including a brief boxing exhibition between Earlie Thomas and our Ken Parker, but football players trying to fight in full uniform are akin to a demolition derby with Patton tanks. It's hard to hurt each other, no matter how hard they try. However, in this particular case, it was like a massive spring unwinding for the Giants. That was what we needed. It was like uncorking a champagne bottle. Our defense rushed onto the field, and Jim Files broke through on the first play and slammed Chuck Mercein to the ground for a safety. They punted to us and we busted back down the field to their 9-yard line. I called a "Y-sneak pass" in which Bob Tucker made a strong block on the defensive end and Tucker Frederickson swung behind him, taking the strong safety and the cornerback with him. Just as it looked as if Bob were out of the play, he recovered from the blocking action and angled into the middle. I hit him on the 3-yard line and we had the lead 12–10. After we kicked off to the Jets, Al Woodall tried a long pass. Willie Williams made a beautiful interception and returned the ball to their 29. A face-masking penalty moved us to the 14. On third and 7, Clifton did a perfect little square-out on Earlie Thomas and took the ball in to make it 19–10. With less than two minutes we'd scored 16 points. Pete Gogolak added 3 more in the last quarter, but it didn't make any difference. The Jets were dead from the moment that that fight began.

We'd won it and it was terribly important. We stood 1–0 against the Jets officially and they would have no chance to face us again for four seasons. Until then, no final settlement about the unofficial City Championship could be made. But even more significant, we'd kept our winning streak alive *and*, best of all, rather than blowing a second-half lead, we'd come back to win.

Game Eight
GIANTS VS. DALLAS COWBOYS
Yankee Stadium, New York City
Sunday afternoon, November 8, 1970
Giants record: 4–3

For the first time since 1963, New York was excited about its Giants. With the increase of interview requests for everybody on the team and the shouted greetings from cab-drivers, construction workers and pedestrians as you walked down the street, the interest was obvious. The Giants were winners, and Manhattan, unlike any other place I know, opened up in a vast display of affection. New York is known as a nasty, insolent town where everybody hates everybody else. Nothing could be farther from the truth with its sports scene. There are many cities in the NFL where a team could win everything except control of the state legislature and nobody would pay the slightest attention to the players. Not so with New York, where suddenly everybody associated with the Giants was being treated like a conquering hero.

We were confident—as only a loose gang of upstarts can be confident, I suppose—that the Cowboys could be beaten. We'd nearly done it in Dallas, and now we were much more potent, both on offense and defense. Dallas had changed, too. Their defense had toughened considerably (if that was possible), but most important, their offensive strength was increasing, mainly because Craig Morton seemed to be gaining confidence at quarterback and Bob Hayes had come out of the management's dog house (which he'd been in for much of the year due to a number of disagreements with the owners and coaches) and was playing at his peak again.

We knew Dallas would be hard to run against, so we decided to rely on a tightly disciplined passing game, coupled with the use of numerous sets and formations to upset their complicated defensive key system. We worked hard on our offense all day Thursday and were about to leave the field when we decided to experiment with one more play. Only Ron Johnson, Clifton McNeil and myself stuck around to practice it, because we were the basic participants in its execution. I'd used a similar set several times in a Vikings-Cowboys exhibition game a number of years earlier and it had worked beautifully. Since the Cowboys' defensive key system had remained essentially unchanged and was based on the proposition that when a pair of offensive receivers operate in the same zone, if the inside man goes inside, the outside man will go outside. We worked on the play, named "Brown right, double wing, X-A post," for about five minutes, just the three of us in the deepening shadows of Yankee Stadium. It worked this way: We used a basic double-wing setup except that Clifton lined up like a tight end on the weak side, with Ron Johnson just off Clifton's right hip. At the snap they both went downfield, Clifton about 8 yards, Ron about 9 yards, and both cut inside. Maybe, just maybe, the Cowboys would bite on such a play.

The passing game didn't work. The Cowboys' front four weren't using their customary flex at all; they were lining up head to head on our linemen and blowing through with all their prodigious speed and strength. I was rushing my passes and we simply weren't moving. Then Morton got the ball to Hayes twice, first for a 38-yard touchdown, then for an 80-yard score that Willie Williams came within a whisker of knocking astray. With the clock moving toward the end of the half we were behind 17–6, and if there is one thing you don't want to do with a hot defensive team like the Cowboys, it's get far behind. Then you are forced to pass deep, looking for quick touchdowns, which is exactly the tactic their pass rushers and secondary men love best. On the last play of the half, Pete Gogolak punched out a 54-yard field goal, the longest in Giant history, to send us off the field only 8 points behind and with a boost in our spirits. Gogy's kick had been a positive action and it convinced us that we could come back and win.

Mike Clark kicked another field goal early in the third quarter to make it 20–9, but it didn't make that much difference. We'd switched to a running game and time and again Ron Johnson broke loose for big gains. He was to finish the game with 136 yards' rushing. We went 71 yards, with Ron scoring from 4 yards out to make it 20–16. Then "Mean Joe" Green recovered an on-sides kick and Ronnie's running again powered us to a first down on the Dallas 2 yard line. But the Cowboys got to me for a pair of 10-yard losses while trying to pass and Pete missed a 27-yard field goal attempt.

The game stabilized for the opening half of the final quarter; then with about five minutes left we took over deep in our territory. This was it: We had to drive for a touchdown or it was probably all over—disregarding some improbable twist of luck. Clifton, who'd broken his nose early in the game, started it off with a great 32-yard-pass reception of a ball I'd tossed a bit high. From there we charged down to the 13 yard line, where it became third down and 6. We had two more chances to make 6 yards and score. A field goal would not help. I called a pass play in the huddle and we were about to break when I yelled, "Wait a minute!" The team gathered around me again and I said, "O.K., here's the play. Brown right, double-wing X and A post on 2." We set up, knowing that Dallas was expecting a pass and readying ourselves for a blitz by holding Bob Tucker and Tucker Frederickson back for additional protection.

Johnson and McNeil streaked downfield in tandem with Cowboys Charley Waters and Mel Renfro in close company. McNeil darted inside and Waters went with him. Ron gave Renfro a perfect fake to the outside and for an instant he was alone in the swirl of bodies. I rifled the ball low and hard and it reached Ron's arms a particle of a second before Renfro recovered and leaped back into position. Ron went into the end zone with the ball high in the air and as Slugger and Gogolak came on the field to convert the extra point that would make it 23–20, I jogged toward the bench thinking that for all the exquisite complexity of the Dallas defense, the proper execution of a simple play could still beat them.

It was a beautiful sound to hear, 62,000 Giants fans chanting, "Defense, defense, defense" as our guys took to the field in one final effort to shut off a Dallas comeback. The Giants' defensive eleven had been sensational that day, holding the Cowboys' great runners to a mere 102 yards and playing excellently against the pass (disregarding the two lapses with the great Bob Hayes, which is inclined to happen to any defense). They were superb and they held in the face of the final Dallas onslaught and there we were, tied for second place in our division, one game behind St. Louis and carrying a five-game winning streak. It was good, but the best was yet to come.

Game Nine
GIANTS VS. WASHINGTON REDSKINS
Yankee Stadium, New York City
Sunday afternoon, November 15, 1970
Giants record: 5–3

The Washington Redskins were a very difficult team to evaluate. Blessed with a fine offense built around Sonny Jurgensen, they seemed to alternate between periods of sheer brilliance and substantial incompetence. Vince Lombardi, prior to his tragic and premature death, had stabilized them somewhat, but he had failed to turn them into the iron-clad warriors many observers had expected. The reason was simple, I believe. Lombardi had achieved his miracles at Green Bay because he had extraordinary personnel who were being used ineffectively before he arrived. People forget that All-Pros Bart Starr, Paul Hornung, Willie Davis, Fuzzy Thurston, etc., were already at Green Bay before Lombardi came to the coaching job, and he was able to galvanize them into a powerhouse. In other words, he had the horsepower waiting for him at Green Bay, but not at Washington. If there is any justice or solace to be found in Lombardi's death, it is that he died with his legend intact. If he had spent a few more seasons at Washington, struggling to energize an under-manned team, his image as a supercoach who could turn anybody, even a random collection of interior decorators, into champions might have been tarnished.

If anything, the most erratic, unpredictable part of Washington's game lay with the defense. They could be over-whelming and in fact as we headed for our first game against them, they had given up a mere 140 points, only 10 more than the conference-leading Cardinals and four more than ourselves. Nevertheless, they were capable of going to pieces at unexpected moments and we felt this weakness could be exploited. The Redskins' record stood at 4 and 4, leaving them still in contention. and the week before they had out-played the Vikings for most of the afternoon before losing 19–10. We thought we could beat them with a minimum of tricks, merely sticking with solid offense and defense designed to keep Jurgensen under rein and their defense pressured to a point where they might begin to make mistakes.

As in so many games, the first half was inconclusive. We led 14–12, but that meant nothing after Jurgensen got his offense operating smoothly in the third quarter. We stood by helplessly as Charlie Harraway ran off tackle 57 yards to score once; then Sonny caught Charlie Taylor with a 28-yard touchdown pass and finally, with twenty-two seconds left in the period, Harraway finished off a lengthy ground assault with a 2-yard run to escalate the score to 33–14. They might as well have been alone on the field for all the resist-ance the Giants offered throughout that unbelievable period. But somehow, call it madness if you like, we opened the fourth quarter still convinced we could win. Alex strode up and down the sidelines announcing that if they could score three touchdowns in the third, we could score three touch-downs in the fourth!

We started carefully, controlling the ball for thirteen plays and 71 yards as we short-passed and ran to their 5 yard line. From there Ron Johnson scooted in and the score was 33–21. Less than two minutes later we had the play that turned it around. We tried a pass that Tucker Frederickson had never practiced—an old pattern we'd used for years at Minnesota and one that's in most of the playbooks in the league. We set up strong right, with Ron Johnson getting a fake handoff while Bob Tucker went out 5 yards and cut toward the middle. In the meantime Tucker Frederickson had headed outside, then cut up the sidelines with man-to-man coverage on the outside linebacker. He got clear by a few steps and I hit him. A few seconds later Tucker barreled into the end zone, having bucked and dodged his way 57 yards to our fourth touchdown. It was one of 10 passes he caught that afternoon for 165 yards, giving him one of the finest days of his career and removing any doubt that he was one of the best fullbacks in pro football. The first man to reach him after he scored and to give him a great hug was Ron Johnson, Tucker's backfield mate and the man Tucker had blocked for so diligently all year.

We had seven minutes left to score once more, and nobody was more impatient than the defense. They bolted into the field and flayed away at the Redskins like wild men. Jurgensen tried to keep his team moving, failed, and they were forced to punt. Bobby Duhon got the ball back to our 27. A third-down, 20-yard pass to Bob Tucker advanced the ball to the Redskin 45; then Tucker Frederickson took another pass to their 32. Two minutes remained and the crowd was going crazy. Chants and cheers rumbled inside the old stadium, making it hard to hear. Banners waved. The place was swirling with excitement. We bogged down and it was fourth and 6 yards to go. A field goal was out of the question. We needed 6 yards on a simple, dependable play, perfectly executed. I called Old Faithful, "13 pass, A-option" the circle pass that had worked so well in the past except for the disaster in the Chicago game earlier in the season. This time Ron Johnson would run the pattern instead of Joe Morrison. It's strange, the things that go through your mind at key moments. As I walked to the line of scrimmage, I thought to myself in a detached way, Man, isn't this some kind of a great game? Here it is, all on the line with this one play. The thought was so isolated from what I was doing that it should have come to me while lounging at home watching the game on television.

Ron broke open for a moment and I got the ball to him even though their middle linebacker, Marlin McKeever, gave him a solid jolt just as the pass reached him. But he held on and tumbled ahead for a 9-yard gain. First down! Another pass to Clifton took us to the 9 and I decided on a running play, then two passes to get us the touchdown. The run would consume more clock and keep the defense off balance, so I called a wide sweep play to the left for Ron, not really expecting a score. Even I underestimated Ron Johnson. A couple of beautiful feints, a few blocks and suddenly he was around the corner. He shouldered off a last-ditch tackle and ran into the end zone, again holding the ball high in the air. Victory!

Gogolak kicked the extra point to make it 35–33 and Yankee Stadium nearly vibrated apart from the sheer tumult of the crowd. With victory still in the grasp of the Redskins via a last-moment field goal, our defense held again, forcing Jurgensen to give up the ball on downs.

Chalk up number six.

Game Ten
GIANTS VS. PHILADELPHIA EAGLES
Franklin Field, Philadelphia
Monday evening, November 23, 1970
Giants record: 6–3

Philadelphia *had* to be better than their record indicated. They'd lost seven games while winning one and tying one, but based on the strength they'd shown us in our first meeting, we were apprehensive about playing the Eagles.

The week before, on the nationally televised Monday evening game, St. Louis had mercilessly stomped Dallas 38–0, giving themselves a tremendous boost in morale and us sole possession of second place. Now it was our turn to perform for the folks across the country, and we knew that Philadelphia was savoring its role as a Giant killer in front of a national television audience. New York and Philadelphia have always been strong rivals in the NFL and both have eagerly contributed to spoiling winning streaks, successful seasons and key games for each other over the years. This was the Eagles' chance and when I entered Franklin Field I knew we were in trouble. The Eagles were being cheered! For years it has been the sole intent of the Eagle fans to abuse their own players. It was almost as if some of them bought tickets completely unaware that another team was present and merely appeared to vent their spleens against the poor Eagles. But on that night they loved them and we were getting the bad reception.

It was the hardest-hitting game we played in the entire season. The Eagles were as tough as they could be, especially

Tim Rossovich, who'd been moved to middle linebacker. There was Tim on practically every play, knocking Giants around with his furry wad of hair bulging out of his helmet and generally raising hell with everything we tried. A high pass from center on a punt attempt gave them the ball on our 1 yard line, which they converted into an early score. As the game moved on, they managed to bottle up Ron Johnson (who sprained his ankle early in the game) and to take the consistency out of our short-passing game. Our special teams gave up long yardage and one cheap touchdown on kick returns. The Eagles dominated the fourth quarter, consuming nearly 10 minutes in an agonizing steady drive that resulted in a touchdown and a 23–20 lead. During the drive they managed to convert three third-and-10 situations into first downs.

We got the ball with a matter of seconds left to score either a tying field goal or a touchdown. We drove to their 45 yard line, where Tucker Frederickson took a screen pass to their 30 and stepped out of bounds with five seconds left. Still time, except the play was called back. The head linesman said our linemen had advanced downfield before the ball was released. He was wrong and the game films proved it. In fact, our linemen were 3 *yards* behind the line of scrimmage when I threw the ball and I am certain his error came because he, not the players, was out of position. The penalty nullified the play and moved us out of field goal range. We lost.

It may sound as if I am blaming the officials for the loss, much as I implied they contributed to our defeat in New Orleans. That's not the case. Philadelphia put 23 points on the scoreboard to our 20, and that was why we lost. However, there's no point in kidding ourselves that officials are infallible. Naturally this sort of talk is heresy among the major domos of the league, who encourage the notion that the officials never make mistakes. That's nonsense and it's useless to delude ourselves to the contrary. They do an excellent job for the most part, but my subjective guess is that officials make mistakes in 5 to 10 per cent of all football plays, either by missing infractions (especially holding by interior linemen) or by judgmental errors in ball placement, close plays at the goal line, etc. It seems that with the availability of instant-replay video tape at all NFL games, a monitor might be set up along the sidelines which the officials could consult before making a final ruling. Now that we have an electronic arbiter available, it seems ridiculous not to take advantage of it, especially when it can be firmly documented that all officials are subject to human error. (In a key late-season game between the Bears and the Rams in 1968, a team of the NFL's top officials missed a complete down and materially influenced the outcome of the game!)

Good officials or bad, right decisions or wrong, the Eagles hit us hard and beat us. The winning streak was over.

But we were still in the race and that's all that counted.

Game Eleven
GIANTS VS. WASHINGTON REDSKINS
Robert F. Kennedy Stadium, Washington, D.C.
Sunday afternoon, November 29, 1970
Giants record: 6–4

No team responds favorably to a loss and there's no question that we were slightly off key for the week following the Philadelphia debacle. And we knew that Washington would be tough, especially in their home park and still fuming over their collapse in Yankee Stadium fourteen days earlier.

It was chilly, gloomy weather when we arrived in Washington on Saturday, which did little to brighten our spirits during practice that afternoon. The evening brought an upturn for me, when Frank Gifford and I were invited to dinner with Sargent Shriver and his wife, Eunice. Ethel Kennedy was there, along with Art Buchwald, plus Sargent's assistant, Bill Mullins and their wives. We relaxed in front of the television set watching football, of all things, in this case the Southern California upset of Notre Dame. I got back to the motel by nine thirty, feeling great, and had a long, hard sleep in anticipation of a long, hard game.

I wasn't sharp. My passes were off target both in practice and in the early stages of the game. It got so bad that I finally sought advice from Slugger, who had a kind of golf pro's ability to diagnose passing techniques. He felt that the hard-packed, practically bare turf in RFK Stadium was making it hard for me to plant my right foot and suggested I take an extra split second to set up before throwing. Slowly I worked myself out of the slump and by the end of the third quarter I'd managed a couple of short touchdown passes to Tucker Frederickson and Bob Tucker and we had ourselves what appeared to be a comfortable 24–10 lead. As it turned out, it was about as "comfortable" as Washington's 34–14 lead in New York. Before five minutes of the final quarter had gone by, Jurgensen had passed them to a pair of touchdowns and the score was tied. Again, as in so many pro games, we'd played the first three quarters for show, and now the resolution to the struggle would be made in the final minutes.

The momentum of the game had gone to the Redskins. Their fans, who's been giving them a pretty lusty booing for most of the afternoon, came alive with cheers, adding to the new spirit. We were stopped to the same, "Defense, defense!" chant that our fans had used against Dallas two weeks before and we were forced to punt. Sonny and the 'Skins started upfield again. Then Willie Williams made a sensational interception on our 35 yard line with 3:48 remaining. We could not afford a tie. We *had* to score. With the stands again thundering "Defense!" we moved the ball into their territory. Bobby Duhon had replaced Ron Johnson in the third quarter after Ron's left ankle started to act up again and now it was Bobby's turn to produce a key play. We needed 6 yards and the Redskins smelled pass. I called a sprint draw off the I-formation in which I began to roll out to the right with Tucker Frederickson leading the blocking. Duhon took a couple of steps with us and at the moment it looked as if I was about to throw the ball, I gave it to Bobby. Our line had blocked perfectly and Duhon made perfect use of their efforts. Before the Redskins stopped him he'd gone 38 yards to their 15-yard line. They stiffened there and Pete Gogolak came in to kick his twentieth field goal of the season, tying him with Pat Summerall and Don Chandler for the team record.

With nearly two minutes left, holding a 3-point lead against a man like Sonny Jurgensen and a collection of dangerous receivers such as Washington's hardly inspired confidence. Sure enough, the Redskins started to move. They collected a pair of first downs, then got bottled up with a fourth down and 2 yards to go at our 36. A time-out and a Washington sideline conference with seventeen seconds remaining and their kicker Curt Knight and the field-goal team entered the game. The dangerous part of this situation lay in the holder, none other than Sonny Jurgensen, who could easily fake a kick, stand up and rifle a pass over the heads of our defenders. Jimmy Garrett warned our guys about such a possibility and my thoughts went to those customary Saturday afternoon sessions with "Hecker's Wreckers." "Hecker's Wreckers" were a collection of Giants old-timers, including myself, Joe Morrison, "Slugger," Matt Hazeltine, etc., who worked each Saturday for about half an hour with our special teams. We were the opposition and worked hard to present them with every kind of nutball play they might encounter. We faked punts and field goals, we lateraled, we did everything possible to ready them for uncertainties like Bobby Joe Green's fake-punt and pass in the opener against the Bears.

Ol' Sonny wasn't about to play for a tie. The ball was centered back into his waiting hands and he leaped to his feet, seeking Pat Richter downfield. His arm was cocked when "Mean Joe" Green got to him. Joe had lined up wide to the left side and had aimed everything in his wiry little body at Sonny, pass or kick. He got a hold of Sonny's left arm and spun him around, delaying the pass. Then Otto Brown, another substitute Giant defensive back, arrived on the scene and slammed Jurgensen to the ground.

That was it. We'd won 27–24 and everyone, including the old gaffers on "Hecker's Wreckers," felt they had a share of the victory.

Game Twelve
Giants vs. Buffalo Bills
Yankee Stadium, New York City
Sunday afternoon, December 6, 1970
Giants record: 7–4

It was hard to get up for Buffalo. We'd never played them before, so there was very little way we could develop an emotional involvement with the team. They were from the other end of the state and from the other league. They had won only two games all season, but they were young, inexperienced and blessed with some top-notch talent. They had the makings of a superb football team, but that would have to wait. There was no way they could beat us this time (so we thought) and the hardest thing we had to do all week was to keep our minds on the Bills and off the big showdown with St. Louis the week following.

We thought we could run outside on the Bills, but the light snow, which hindered the footing, and Buffalo's substantially underrated defense canceled any notions of that early in the going. They were using odd defensive alignments that confused our blocking somewhat and we didn't move the ball very well. We were rather flat in the first half and aside from a touchdown pass to Clifton, we showed them very little offense. Fortunately their rookie quarterback, Dennis Shaw, wasn't having a particularly good day either, and their attack was even more feeble than ours. Then Les Shy, whom we'd obtained in a late trade from Dallas, took the second-half kickoff on a jaunt to the Buffalo's 20, and Gogolak scored us a field goal. In the meantime, Alex had decided that we should return to basic inside running plays and we used a pair of them, "power 21" and "power 30," to beat the Bills. On "power 21," Frederickson led the blocking for Ron Johnson into a hole opened by Willie Young and Pete Case on the left side. "Power 30" went to the right, between Doug Van Horn and Rich Buzin. Hardly dazzling football, but these plays gave us control of the ball and ultimate control of the game, 20–6. Like the man said, in the end, it's a simple game.

Next week—the day of reckoning in St. Louis.

Game Thirteen
GIANTS VS. ST. LOUIS CARDINALS
Bush Stadium, St. Louis
Sunday afternoon, December 13, 1970
Giants record: 8–4

I will probably never figure out why we beat St. Louis so badly. They never got a sniff at the lead and we had them 21–0 before they finally managed a field goal. Our defense was great against their power runners and they never really threatened us. Everything worked for us—passing, running, defense, kicking—you name it, and the New York Giants did it against the Cardinals (Bob Tucker caught our first touchdown one-handed, for example). *The* Cardinals, were leading our division and were judged to be far and away more powerful than we were. What's more, they were sky-high for the game. I can remember meeting Phil King in the lobby of our motel the day before the game and hearing him recount a midweek St. Louis football awards dinner that turned into a frantic, college-brand pep rally. "Let's chase Howard Cosell and his New York buddies out of town," yelled one booster, forgetting that Howard had sniped a great deal more at the Giants over the years than at the Cardinals, and if anybody was going to run Howard out of town, it might have been us. Stormy Bidwell, whose family owns the Cardinals, stood up and proclaimed, "We're going to show the New York press that people can play football west of the Mississippi, too!" Even Larry Wilson, whom I've known for years, got carried away with the fervor of the moment and pleaded, "Let's stick the ball in Fran Tarkenton's ear!" (It being a public gathering, Larry chose my ear, although I'm inclined to think that in the privacy of the locker room, he'd have opted for some other orifice).

We listened to a broadcast of the final quarter of the Dallas-Cleveland game in the locker room following our late Saturday-afternoon practice. The Cowboys managed to extract a 6–2 victory from the muddy, bruising contest, meaning we had to win against the Cardinals the next afternoon. Sportswriters were noting that we had never won a game on artificial turf. Bush Stadium had artificial turf and the Cardinals were unbeaten on artificial turf. In the six games since we had scored 5 touchdowns against the Cardinal defense, they'd let their goal line be crossed only three times. They had shut out three teams in a row, a record. This was supposed to be an omen that the Giants were going to get thrashed. They forgot one thing: We were loose, the Cardinals were tight. In our last two meetings, with essentially their same personnel, we'd pounded them 49–6 and 35–17. What's more, if there is anything to the thesis that one team can get another's number (and I'm not sure there is), then we had St. Louis' number. Since the Giants' first meeting in 1926 with the then Chicago Cardinals, we'd beaten them forty-one times with one tie. They'd won but fifteen.

We streamed onto the field to find the first full house I'd ever seen in St. Louis. Every seat seemed filled with a screaming, hooting Giants hater. They booed so loudly when we appeared that half the Star-Spangled Banner was drowned out by the noise. This sort of thing, along with the chatter in the papers, really doesn't make much difference. Crowds can give you something of a boost if they're with you, but a professional athlete becomes so calloused to booing that it simply doesn't penetrate his consciousness after a while. If you are really concentrating, only the events on the playing field have any impact on you whatsoever.

We had superiority almost immediately. The defense held perfectly, refusing to let the Cardinals convert but two of their ten third-down plays into first downs. MacArthur Lane, their number-one frontline runner, who had been the league's leading rusher for much of the season, gained 26 yards. We had twenty more offensive plays than they did, a solid indication of the lopsided nature of the contest. Excluding three long touchdown plays, a 79-yard screen pass to Lane, a 48-yard pass to Jackie Smith and a 33-yarder to John Gilliam, the Cardinals went nowhere.

Everything worked for us. During the opening series of plays, we'd worked some pitch-outs to Johnson, trying to gain big yardage on the outside. At one point Tucker Frederickson entered the huddle and announced, "The 'give' is there." Those were big words for Tucker, because he hated the "give," an old play that required the defensive tackle to pursue a pulling guard, thereby leaving a hole in the center of the line. The old Lombardi Packers had used a "double give" to perfection, wherein each guard would pull to the opposite side of the field and the defensive tackles would follow, leaving an avenue up the middle about as wide as the San Bernadino Freeway. But the defensive tackles *had* to take the bait, otherwise they would be waiting in perfect position for the runner. I can remember calling a Double Give against the 49ers while I was with Minnesota. I spun and gave the ball to poor old' Bill Brown and then heard this great *thump-oof* sound. I turned around to see Bill lying in a dazed heap at the feet of San Francisco's immense defensive tackles, Charlie Krueger and Roland Lakes, neither of whom had chased our pulling guards! Bill wouldn't speak to me for a week after that play. Tucker had a preservation instinct strong enough to be wary of "give" plays for this very reason. However, he'd been watching the Cardinal's Bob Rowe on each of the earlier pitch-outs and noticed that Rowe, a fleet 255-pounder, had been charging in furious pursuit of our own Pete Case. I called the give, Case pulled, Rowe followed and Frederickson burst up the middle for 40 yards. It was that kind of day.

At the end of it, with the score a giddy 34–17, the grandstands, once full of furious Cardinal rooters, were half-empty. Those who remained sat in stunned silence. Finally all the taunts, pushing and shoving that had been going on among the players erupted into a last-minute fight. It was broken up without serious consequences and we sprinted off the field, having played our first game for first place since 1963.

The New York Giants had knocked the Cardinals out of first and we now shared that rather lofty, unfamiliar position with the Cowboys. The mathematical possibilities were complicated, but it boiled down to this: If we could take our last game against the Rams, we were in the playoffs.

Of the Giants' starters, only Willie Williams, Jim Kanicki, Clifton McNeil and Ron Johnson had ever played in a postseason playoff game.

Game Fourteen
GIANTS VS. LOS ANGELES RAMS
Yankee Stadium, New York City
Sunday afternoon, December 20, 1970
Giants record: 9–4

"The Commander" took over as my nursemaid the week before the Rams game. I moved into Manhattan so that

I could concentrate completely on preparations, and Neil made sure I was sent home and in bed by eleven o'clock each night, except for Monday, when we gathered for a wild bachelor party for Bobby Duhon, who was to marry Tucker's sister, Mary Ann Frederickson, a Pan Am stewardess, as soon as the season was over. We had fun, but it was football that dominated the affair. We watched the ABC night game in which the Detroit Lions gave the Rams a solid whipping. Although we were pleased at the outcome, it was to effect our game. Maxie Baughan, the ex-Rams' linebacker, who lives near me in Atlanta, told me later that the humiliation at the hands of the Lions sent the Rams into New York as a mean, surly football team bent on salvaging their reputation. And like the Giants, they had a chance of making the playoffs if they beat us while their arch-rivals, San Francisco, lost to Oakland.

It was slightly more complicated for us. A win would give us the title in the Eastern Division of the NFL no matter if Dallas won their final game or not (simply because our inter-divisional record of 6–2 was better than Dallas' 5–3). A tie would be acceptable *if* Dallas did no better than a tie against Houston. This, however, was unlikely. Houston was completing a terrible 3–9–1 season, and the Cowboys were 12-point favorites to beat them—meaning we had to win. If we lost both the Cardinals, who were playing Washington, and Dallas would have to lose for us to win the title. That was more than anybody could hope for. It was up to us.

The game films of the Rams' front four made one pause to wonder. Without question Merlin Olsen and David Jones, their two headliners, were as powerful and agile as any defenders in football, but it was their two lesser-known partners, Coy Bacon and Diron Talbert, who surprised me. They looked overwhelming and I knew our handyman Charlie

Harper, who was filling in for the second week for the injured Willie Young (ankle sprain), was going to have his hands full with Bacon, who was four inches taller and twenty pounds heavier. What's more, Charlie simply hadn't played tackle much, making his task border on the impossible. The films left me even more convinced that when they were at their best, Los Angeles ranked with Kansas City and Minnesota as the toughest, most physically aggressive and punishing team in football.

If we were to beat them, a running game had to be established. Otherwise their great pass rush could be brought to bear with full force and that spelled disaster. Although Jones was one of the greatest outside pass rushers in football, some felt he had weaknesses against the run, which made it even more important that we establish this part of our game. Their offense wasn't as potent as it had been in years past, meaning that if we could squeeze out an early lead and maintain some momentum on the ground, we had a chance.

The game breaker came early. With the score 0–0, I tried a bootleg action pass in which Ronnie and Tucker Frederickson went right while I rolled left. Tucker got free and I spotted him in the clear at the Rams' 25 with an open field ahead. I threw the ball over his head. I wasn't rushed, I wasn't troubled, I just threw the blasted thing over his head. Instead of a 7–0 lead, which would have done wonders for our confidence, we had to settle for a field goal (which in a sense is a victory for the opposition). From there Roman Gabriel hit Jack Snow with a long pass that led to their first touchdown and a lead they never gave up. They held us, then mounted another assault that resulted in Jerry Shay's breaking his leg. They carried Jerry off the field on a stretcher and everyone in the hushed stadium felt that the Giants' season was going with him. Without his bulldog play in the middle, our defense lost steam, and the Rams scored twice more with ease.

That put us exactly where we didn't want to be—having to shoot for touchdowns. That meant passing, which in the face of Olsen, Jones, Bacon and Talbert, was something akin to trying to pass in a subway during rush hour. Time and again they thundered through us, hurrying my passes, forcing me to lob the ball over their outstretched arms and flopping me to earth like a rag doll. Once this begins to happen, once one team gets the upper hand and the other begins to press, the score can get outlandish. Our successes over St. Louis involved this situation, wherein the winner gets better and the loser gets worse, boosting the score to absurd margins. There are games, and ours against Los Angeles and St. Louis were two, wherein the score bore no indication of the relative quality of the two teams. One team was up, the other down, and the outcome was hopelessly distorted. Both games produced big winners and big losers. We were both—heroes against the Cardinals, bums against the Rams. Play the two games again, and the outcome might be exactly reversed. That's the fascinating enigma in sports.

But on that Sunday in Yankee Stadium, as we say, the Rams whipped our asses. Until then there had been hope. It was over.

VIII

THERE WAS NO REASON to punch lockers, heave helmets or kick equipment bags. We'd tried and we'd come close, we'd turned a lot of heads, surprised a lot of people, but in the end it hadn't taken us anywhere. Dallas had bombed Houston on that final day and embarked on a two-game playoff streak that took them to the Super Bowl. Maybe, just maybe, that would have been us. But in the end it wasn't, and 1970 will record the New York Giants as having finished at nine wins and five losses, enough for second place in the Eastern Conference of the National Conference of the National Football League. It brought us no extra playoff money, few extra accolades and little more artistic satisfaction than having Ron Johnson become the Giants' first thousand-yard rusher in history and, with myself, one of two representatives on the NFL Pro Bowl team. Alex was presented with several honors, including a Coach of the Year selection by the Washington Touchdown Club.

What did come to us was a new feeling of self, a new sense of purpose and hope for the Giants. For the first time in seven seasons, the Giants were contenders, actually in the thick of it until the very end. We finished the season as winners for the first time in seven years and we left for our

178

homes with the feeling that sometime within the playing careers of all of us we would bring a championship to New York. Ultimately it was hope that triumphed during those fourteen Sundays—or should I say one Saturday, twelve Sundays and one Monday? Either way, it was the best season I'd ever spent in football.

Nineteen seventy also brought to the fore a spate of hard truth about major league professional sports, producing powerful indictments about racism, profiteering, dehumanization and drugs. Suddenly America's heroes were being described as sadistic, mainlining animals, with no regard for anything except profit and their precious bodies. I'm sure I would make many friends inside the football establishment if I made a fervent denial of these charges, doing my best to defend the myth for generations of small boys to come—like the little kid who implored Joe Jackson during the Black Sox scandal many years ago: "Say it ain't so, Joe." As it turned out, it was so, partially at least, and it still is partially so. Of course there are abuses and stupidity and avarice spread throughout the game, but to leave it at that is to distort the picture as much as some hack sportswriters who slavishly portray every jock as a clean-living defender of the American way. Both extremes are nonsensical.

Dave Meggysey, a former linebacker for the St. Louis Cardinals, has attacked football as representing the "death culture" while gaining a great deal of notoriety by writing a book called *Out of My League*. Johnny Sample, a cornerback for the Colts and the Jets, has produced a book in which he candidly admits that the two things that made him an extraordinary football player were his penchant for dirty play and his abrasive personality, then blasts the sport for removing him from action on the basis of some shadowy "quota" conspiracy. Chip Oliver, a fine Oakland Raiders linebacker, didn't bother to write a book but merely quit football to join the hippie community around Berkeley, California. He has publicly denounced pro football and claims that yoga exercises and long mountain runs are real athletic endeavors, as opposed to "puritantical, anti-body" attitudes exemplified by most organized sports. On a Public Broadcasting Network documentary called "Take Me Out of the Ball Game" Oliver said, "When you make the final score the ultimate goal, the players forget how they play in between and the means doesn't matter, only the end. . . . Competition fails when you set up a reward. . . . It's freedom that we need, that's what'll heal humanity, get out from under the thumb of all the authorities."

Ah, freedom and pure atheltics. What a wonderful pure state of being. The same TV show carried some footage of a pickup game in a park at Berkeley, labeled the "Freak Bowl," in which Oliver and some friends were supposed to demonstrate the unsullied glories of good-fun, no-reward sandlot football. Two little ironies came to me as I watched the game: (1) no blacks were shown on either team (surely there can't be any "racism" in a "pure" contest like that, can there?) and (2), Chip Oliver appeared to be acting as the quarterback of one team, doing most of the running and passing. Very likely Chip was the best athlete on the field, but to use him in the key offensive position? That can't mean they were trying to—*win*? Heaven forbid! Aren't winning and "rewards" all part of the evil system?

In a recent speech at Syracuse University, his alma mater, Meggysey said, the keynote of the "death culture" is ". . . competition, and emphasis on product, and emphasis on winning (score those touchdowns); an emphasis on military victories, not humane rational solutions. The life culture is trying to say something else. It's saying, instead of competition, let's talk about cooperation, working together . . . yes, product is important, but the process is equally important, not the goddam grades, it's the process of how much you put into it and how much comes back to you. Instead of alienation comes a process of coming together, living together, working together, sharing energy and getting high together. . . ."

Of course a certain percentage of the less-secure academic community have found a great deal of comfort in such statements. And I suppose I can't blame them, because they've always been a bit intimidated, in a sheer physical sense, by the presence of burly jocks within the cloistered halls of their universities. Of all the disputes on the American education scene, this rift between the so-called jocks and the so-called intellectuals is the most idiotic, with a vast amount of misunderstanding on each side constantly fueling the argument. Meggysey and Oliver have given the anti-jocks some potent ammunition, but I think the entire issue is absurd. Of course there are cruelties and exploitation on the major league athletic scene—just as there are cruelties and exploitation within the *academe* and the hippie world. They are evil and should be corrected and, I think, in a sense, the rather simplistic, Pollyanna statements of men like Oliver and Meggysey may help in the long run to remedy the situation. However I cannot accept the general theme of anti-athletic critics that all big league sport is cryto-fascist and alien to civilization.

Like it or not, as Lord Kenneth Clark has observed, all great civilizations have been physically and mentally aggressive. Western man has constantly tested and retested his courage and resourcefulness in a countless variety of ways, and a number of the tests have involved athletic prowess. Inevitably these tests have led to a distillation process whereby the very best in a given field of endeavor have been pitted against each other to determine the best of the best, so to speak. Athletic tests that lead to the Super Bowl or high school essay contests that lead to the National Book Awards relate to essentially the same thing—man's search to quantify and catalogue his best efforts. Unfortunately these endeavors bring forth the best and worst motives in man—as does practically everything he undertakes. But no matter how strident the cries for unstructured "freedom," contests and competition, both conscious and unconscious, will remain an integral part of civilization until man establishes more subtle ways to measure worth and progress.

Athletes are people—people subject to every possible human failing. Within the National League, for example, I am sure you could find some of the worst people on the face of the earth. I think you could also find some of the best, depending on the criteria by which you judge them.

If somebody chooses to call the rigid training that a professional athlete must endure dehumanizing, that is his choice, based on a certain point of view. However, I am inclined to think that every harsh regimen of the mind and body might be described as dehumanizing. What about ballet? In this exquisitely graceful art form, the participants are forced to undergo some of the most arduous training known to man. Is this dehumanizing? Is a ballet master more heartless than a football coach? Is a concert violinist or pianist forced to suffer more degradation than a professional football player? Is a student figure skater driven as close to limits of endurance as a young football player? These questions can be answered only once one has established priorities and made a rigid determination that one endeavor is more important than the other. I am not prepared to try to give such answers.

Of course drugs are used in the National Football League.

"Uppers" of all sorts—Benzedrine, Dexedrine, etc.—are widely used, especially among the defensive linemen, to provide a final plateau of endurance and competitive zeal. They are not taken for fun, for escape or some hedonistic frolic; they are consumed to raise the level of skill, and make no mistake about it, for certain tasks requiring short, intense bursts of energy, they may work. (It could be that much of the boost they provide is psychological not physical.) I am not endorsing their usage, I am merely acknowledging their existence. Now we might decide that this is despicable, that professional athletes have no right to operate other than in a perfectly straight frame of mind; yet we turn around and tacitly accept the fact that most great pop musicians are stoned out of their minds when they perform—and in fact some of the strongest critics of pro football actively condone the use of grass, etc., by the heroes of the so-called new culture. I do not use drugs on or off the field and I never have, but I do object to the condemnation of professional athletics in this regard by people who defend drug use in other walks of life. We shed a tear for Dylan Thomas or F. Scott Fitzgerald because they drank too much, but vilify an athlete because he uses a chemical to increase his efficiency. At the very least it is *all* wrong and in the end reflects a weakness on the part not of certain individuals or certain professions but of society itself.

Surely no one can deny that pro football is infested with profiteers, that the lofty images of "pure sport" have been bastardized in the lust for money. I can remember my irritation with the Giants when they took out a one-million-dollar life insurance policy on me with themselves as beneficiaries! If I was worth that much, I commented, it seemed only right that I be paid that much. The reply was self-explanatory: they were only protecting their investment. Nobody in professional football likes being depreciated annually, like a hydraulic press or an oil well, but there it is, raw finance in the wonderful world of sport. And if you want to play, you learn to swallow these little indignities. And why do you want to play? Because in the end it is fun. I can't think of many successful professional players who didn't love what they were doing. No man would be able to take such a physical and mental lashing year in and year out without loving it. Why we love it—the competition, the *camaraderie*, the emotional peaks and valleys—is another question entirely, but the fact remains that there are several thousand men in the United States with enough physical skill and mental desire to battle on a grass field for fourteen Sunday afternoons for the highest possible stakes. And in this particular moment in history those stakes involve money.

Racism? I think I can speak with reasonable authority on that subject. One of the greatest compliments of my life was paid to me last year by Spider Lockhart, one of the best men I've ever met. He said, "Fran, You've got to be one of us. Under the thin layer of white skin, you're pure black." I have four members on the board of directors of Tarkenton Ventures. One is black. He is not there as an act of tokenism or to salve my conscience. He is there because he can do the job. I trust him and I respect him. His color means nothing. He is a man. That is all that counts.

I am sure there have been acts of racial prejudice in the NFL. After all, there have been acts of racial prejudice in every other phase of life, so why should football be expected to be innocent? However, I believe that the whining of some black activists about quotas, blacklisting, the absence of black quarterbacks, etc., stands as the biggest cop-out and greatest disservice to advancement of the cause of black men in sports which I can imagine. Although I can only speak for the two teams with which I have been involved, the Minnesota Vikings and the New York Giants, I will say that the idea that these teams employed blacks on the basis of a "quota" is idiotic. Professional football is the ultimate of pragmatism; either you can do the job or you can't. The record is there on the field and on the game films. If you can help the team win, you will stay; if somebody can do your job better, it is likely you will go; and it makes no difference if you're related to George Wallace or Eldridge Cleaver. Produce and you play, it's that simple.

A coach is hired to create winning teams, nothing else. It is madness to accept the premise that a professional coach would cut a black player who could help him win merely to maintain some hazy quota system. He is accountable to a public and a press that don't give a damn about anything except winning, and a coach's attributing his failure to a necessity for maintaining a certain color level on his team should get him committed to an institution. The same goes for players. We are accountable only for winning. In 1970 I had two outside receivers, Clifton McNeil, who is black, and Don Herrmann, who is white. I threw more balls to Clifton during the season than I did to Don. If that had been the reverse, would I have been guilty of racial prejudice? The question is too absurd to deserve an answer.

When I first came into pro football with the Vikings, I was extremely conscious of trying to work with my black teammates. I'd never played on any permanent basis with blacks before and I wanted very badly to make it clear to them that I wasn't a bigot. In so doing I overcompensated and began to give some of the black guys special treatment. I quickly discovered that this was ridiculous; that they merely asked to be treated like *men*, no more, no less, and since those early days of adjustment I've tried to deal with every one of the Vikings and the Giants as men, not as blacks and whites.

I suppose it was a natural development, but I'm convinced that the new rise in black activism in sports has somewhat complicated the racial situation in pro football. I can remember that in my first few years with the Vikings we all socialized with one another, drank together, ate together, went to the movies together. But that has changed; now that the black players have become more conscious of themselves and their racial heritage. It's sad in a way, because now the Giants' training tables, except for guys like Spider Lockhart and myself, are largely split down racial lines—whites with whites, blacks with blacks. We room together on road trips in similar fashion, although this is done on the basis of personal friendships and the choice is voluntary. Some teams establish roommates alphabetically, but the Giant players' council, made up blacks and whites, unanimously agree that a better system permits as many friends as possible to share rooms on trips. Although the old black-white mingling looked better on the surface, it was really a scab over a terrible sore that had been festering in this country for a century. At least today that scab has been rubbed away and I think now that the wound is exposed to fresh air it will heal. Today we may have more superficial separation of the races on football teams than ever before, but the situation is constantly improving as the black players drive forward to establish their rightful sense of pride and dignity. We've come a long way. We'll go a lot farther.

There may have been stronger racial splits on other teams because of the new awareness and activism of black athletes and the reaction of old-line whites. It would seem a natural thing, owing to the upsets we have encountered throughout society, but I am inclined to think that such splits have been exaggerated. After all, there are few better examples of black and white men working toward a common goal, side by side, down there in the mud together, than in professional athletics. When all the recriminations are over, I think the record is pretty good compared to that of most of society.

No black quarterbacks you say? Not yet, but they are on their way. Marlin Briscoe had his chance at Denver. Jimmy Harris started a number of games for Buffalo, and Eldridge Dickey may yet make it at Oakland. The fact is that no black man has come along with the *clear-cut* skill to take over a starting quarterback job in the NFL, and until that day comes (which it will) the sport will be subjected to this ludicrous indictment. I can only make this retort: A vast majority of the cornerbacks and safety men in the league, something like 85 per cent, are black. If some fool can accuse the system of racism for the absence of black quarterbacks, isn't it just as guilty of reverse racism because there aren't many white secondary men?

It's difficult to speculate on the reasons, because very little research has been done on the subject, but there seems to be a relationship between the positions men play and their ethnic and racial backgrounds. It can be generalized that most offensive linemen are white, and numerous defensive linemen, in addition to the aforementioned cornerbacks, are black (although my personal candidates for all-time great linemen, offensive tackle Jim Parker and defensive tackle Bob Lilly, perfectly contradict this thesis). Many back activists have charged that there is no Negro middle linebacker because Whitey has kept this prestigious spot open for himself. This is foolishness again, disproved in part by black middle linebacker Willie Lanier of the Kansas City Chiefs and by Marion Motley, considered by some to be the greatest all-around player in history, who played the position for the Cleveland Browns before the two-platoon system was adopted. If this racist statement is correct, it would seem logical that the white establishment would also go to great lengths to keep black players out of the backfield, where runners operate knee-deep in glory and adulation. Why then have men like Jim Brown, Gale Sayers, Joe Perry, Leroy Kelly, Ron Johnson, Calvin Hill, Jim Nance, Bobby Mitchell, Cookie Gilchrist, Lenny Moore, Don Perkins and countless others been permitted to gain the exposure that supposedly was being reserved for the li 'ol white boys? Why? Because they all brought unique talents to the game which helped their teams win, nothing more, nothing less.

It may be that the black athlete has particular physical skills and ethnic behavior patterns that suit him perfectly to the demands for agility, speed and strength made on both cornerbacks and running backs. At the same time I wonder why so many truly great linebackers such as Ray Nitschke, Dick Butkus, Nick Buoniconti, Mike Lucci, Joe Fortunato and others have come from Italian and Middle European backgrounds. Is there something in their physical and mental makeup that qualifies them for that curious brand of "hold the fort" aggressiveness required by the position? I don't know, but it might seem more than circumstantial that so many men from similar origins have gravitated to the top in this particular job.

As for quarterback, it doesn't take more than a few seconds of glancing at the NFL rosters to figure out that a vast majority of them are Anglo-Saxons. Again, a hurried indictment might be made on the basis that the WASP establishment is saving the "best" for themselves, but that is so stupid a charge that it barely deserves reply. As I said, a number of blacks have been tried as quarterback by a number of teams and there is no question that they would have won the assignment *if* they'd been able to get the job done. Here again, a certain subjective opinion of mine comes up, which has nothing to do with race but does relate to cultural background. By tradition, Anglo-Saxons have been prideful, explorative, curious, men with a powerful strain of self-confidence. These characteristics have been developed over centuries of family life and schooling, and Anglo-Saxons seem to be ethnically well equipped to operate as leaders. On the other hand, the hatred and cultural isolation meted out to the Black man over the past centuries seem to have provided an environment far removed from that in which cocky, quarterback types are fostered. Therefore, as the black community gains confidence in itself (which is happening at an ever accelerating rate), it should begin to raise the kind of whip-cracking personalities who can ramrod around a collection of diverse personalities like a football team. So far, for better or for worse, the Anglo-Saxon seems best equipped —culturally, not physically—for this job. If ethnic background has no relationship to sport, then please tell me where the Jewish football players are, or what happened to the waves of Irish prize fighters who used to dominate boxing? Obviously it has nothing to do with athletic skills—after all, Sid Luckman, one of the greatest quarterbacks in history, was Jewish—but more with those subtle tugs and pulls of cultural forces that shape and mold young men. There's nothing right or wrong about it; it bears no relationship to race or racial prejudice, it merely seems to exist, and the sooner some of the more vocal activists on the racial scene stop copping out and face realities like this, the better the climate in professional sports will be.

Quite frankly, I think the black pro football player is being short-changed only in the matter of pay. Although great stars like Jim Brown and O. J. Simpson certainly made or are making as much as anybody else in the game, I can think of other journeymen black players who are not earning as much as their white counterparts. The reason is probably due to a certain naïveté and lack of experience in bargaining for a contract. Many black players enter the NFL from small Negro colleges without the hoopla and press buildup that a player, white or black, might gain from the flacks associated with a majority university. They come to the pros without high-powered agents and lawyers to negotiate for them and because the owners are under no pressure to offer them a big buck, they tend to sign for less. We can hope that new awareness on the part of the young blacks, together with a stronger Players Association and a more enlightened attitude on the part of the owners, will help to rectify this inequity.

If we are going to deal intelligently with the subject of minority groups and pro football, first we've got to be serious and all the bilge being passed around about who-can-and-who-can't play what position is hardly serious. Just one final note on the subject: Probably the most respected and influential man among all the players in the NFL is the president of our Players Association. His name is John Mackey. He is our leader. He is black.

As I have said, professional sport is a mirror of our times. If it does not measure up to the image society has created for it, this is probably the fault of that society. Because we have certain unusual capabilities with regard to our bodies—speed, coordination, strength, size, etc.—we are not necessarily endowed with any extraordinary moral traits. We are human beings, nothing more, nothing less, and our ability to heave a ball into the nickel seats or flatten seven men with a deft block has nothing whatsoever to do with our sense or our sensibilities. It is the public that frequently credits us with extraordinary powers, and it is the public that is often disappointed and angry because we haven't lived up to their fantasies.

Nevertheless, there will always be sports as long as man can walk upright and maintain a sense of self. At least we of the National Football League put on uniforms to play a game and not to kill people. If you think we're a problem now, just think what we'd do if they made us into an army!

See you in the Super Bowl. I'll be the one behind the big guys. Probably running.